MICHIGAN MAN

JIM HARBAUGH AND THE REBIRTH
OF WOLVERINES FOOTBALL

MICHIGAN MAN

JIM HARBAUGH AND THE REBIRTH OF WOLVERINES FOOTBALL

* * *

Angelique Chengelis

Library of Congress Cataloging-in-Publication Data
  Names: Chengelis, Angelique, 1964- author.
  Title: Michigan man: Jim Harbaugh and the rebirth of
    Wolverines football /Angelique Chengelis.
  Description: Chicago, Illinois : Triumph Books LLC, [2017]
  Identifiers: LCCN 2017016997 | ISBN 9781629374161
  Subjects: LCSH: Harbaugh, Jim, 1963- | Football coaches—
    Michigan—Ann Arbor—Biography. | University of
    Michigan—Football—History. | Michigan Wolverines
    (Football team)—History.
  Classification: LCC GV958.U52863 C444 2017 | DDC
    796.332092 [B]—dc23 LC record available at
    https://lccn.loc.gov/2017016997

This book is available in quantity at special discounts for your group or organization. For further information, contact:
  Triumph Books LLC
  814 North Franklin Street
  Chicago, Illinois 60610
  (312) 337-0747
  www.triumphbooks.com

Printed in U.S.A.

ISBN: 978-1-62937-416-1

Design by Florence Aliesch

For David. I am forever grateful for your constant support and encouragement. I could not have done any of this without you.

Contents

Foreword

THE UNIVERSITY OF MICHIGAN HAS BEEN AND CON-
tinues to be a driving, positive, integral part of the Harbaugh
family. Since Jackie and I drove into Ann Arbor in 1973, moved our
three children onto Anderson Avenue, enrolled them into Saint
Francis Assisi Elementary School, and met a man named Bo, our
family has been shaped by this great university and its football program.

Former players, coaches, football staff, faculty, alumni, and fans
come back each fall weekend to share their experiences and tell
their stories with numbing repetition. With each story they attempt
to recapture the magic of those days at the University of Michigan.
For Jackie and me, those meetings with our teammates and friends
on those football weekends goes beyond recognizing a face; it is a
memory being told through a story. Those shared memories bring
us joy and happiness.

What is it that brings us back? The closest I have come to understanding this dynamic is recalling a meeting organized in 1989
to celebrate the long, rich football heritage of Michigan football
and Bo Schembechler's 20 years as Michigan's head football coach.
There were 700 attendees at this prestigious gathering. These men
had coached, played, or worked on the staff for a period extend-
ing from the 1940s through 1989. Each decades group selected a
representative to speak on its behalf. Jim Harbaugh was selected to

speak for the '80s group. Jim was a member of the Chicago Bears and coached by Mike Ditka at the time. He gave no indication as to what he might say, and little did I know that he would answer the aforementioned question. He described through a story why we come back and how Bo and his staff have shaped our lives and the lives of our families.

Jim told the story of the beginning of his third year as a University of Michigan football player in 1984 and his earning the starting quarterback position. The team was opening the season at home against the University of Miami, the defending national champion. Jim had waited his turn and was anxiously counting down the days to kickoff. During idle talk with his position coach, Jerry Hanlon, at the football office on the corner of State and Hoover Streets, he asked an innocent question: "What kind of football team will we have this year?"

Jerry answered, "I don't know."

"What do you mean you don't know? You have coached forever and have been at Michigan for 15 years! Come on," Jim replied.

The next words spoken by Jerry define how the University of Michigan football program was built and how it will be sustained as long as Jim Harbaugh is their head coach. Jerry's answer was: "We won't know how good this football team will be until 15, 20, 25, 30 years from now. Then, we will see what kind of husbands, fathers, providers, community leaders, teammates, and friends you will become. Come back then, and we will know what kind of team you are."

They come back whenever they have the chance. They tell their stories, they laugh, they talk about their families, they brag about their children and grandchildren, and somewhere Bo is smoking a big cigar, smiling, and saying, "They turned out to be a damned good football team." And he is proud of them.

Jackie and I have front-row seats to the program. Or, more accurately, a next-door view because that's where Sarah, Jim, and the kids live. We witness that Jim and his staff are working hard to build good husbands, fathers, providers, community leaders, teammates, and friends through the University of Michigan football experience, and, along the way, win some championships.

—Jack Harbaugh
Michigan assistant coach 1973–79
Father of Jim Harbaugh

Attack this day with an enthusiasm unknown to mankind...

Prologue

A FTER THE 2014 SEASON, ONE THAT FINISHED A DIS-
mal 5–7, saw the firing of head coach Brady Hoke, and the
sudden resignation of athletic director Dave Brandon, the task of
hiring a new coach fell to Jim Hackett, a former Michigan player
under Bo Schembechler and CEO of Steelcase.

Jim Harbaugh became the popular choice among Michigan
fans.

But it seemed the Michigan fans were the only ones who thought
Harbaugh would leave the NFL where he had enjoyed success with
the San Francisco 49ers, including a Super Bowl appearance facing
his brother John's Baltimore Ravens.

Harbaugh's name had been bandied about during previous
searches at Michigan if only for the reason he played quarterback
for the Wolverines under legendary Coach Schembechler, and his
father, Jack, had been an assistant coach on Schembechler's staff
when Jim and John were growing up. But Harbaugh had a proven
coaching record in college and then with the 49ers, so he was by no
means just a sentimental favorite.

The sentiment among NFL insiders and experts, though, was
that Harbaugh would never leave the NFL, even though the pull to
his alma mater could be strong. No way college football, they believed, would be appealing enough for him—not even the Michigan
job.

Hackett wanted to bring Harbaugh to Michigan, but he knew he would have to build a larger candidate pool in case the NFL experts were right about his main target. He and his staff referred to the Michigan football coach hiring process by an amusing code name—"Project Unicorn." In his first detailed comments about the search on *The Huge Show*, Hackett would later say that while they were having some fun with the name, "the unicorn is about perfection. To find something that's perfect."

Then again, he also just really liked referring to it by a ridiculous name. Hackett and his select group worked secretively in the Michigan Stadium suites. They used the "Project Unicorn" reference to keep their work secure and avoid leaks. Although there were other names on the candidate list, Harbaugh was always the No. 1 goal and target. He was the unicorn Hackett wanted.

But this wasn't only about Hackett. The Michigan players were left coachless, and he met with them that December to get a sense for what they were going through and what they wanted. "When Brady had departed and we hadn't hired the coach, I asked for feedback," Hackett told me. "And they said they respect the history, but they wanted to make history. They wanted to be known for something special they did to contribute to the Michigan legacy."

They echoed what Hackett wanted. He wanted to contribute in this way to the Michigan legacy. Jack Harbaugh became an important conduit, considering Jim Harbaugh was still coaching the 49ers through their season. Hackett was determined to make a splash and make this hire. "I didn't want to be denied what was best for Michigan," Hackett said. "That's the way I thought about it. It wasn't Jim Hackett; it was Michigan. This was a cause for me."

Hackett obtained Harbaugh's cell phone number from Jack. "I asked his father if he thought it would be a waste of time given his options," Hackett said. "Jack said, 'Nah, you should talk to him.'"

The initial call was made. "Jim was 10 or 12 when I played, and Jack was the coach that I would talk to often," Hackett said. "I had to reacquaint myself [with Jim]. I called Jim and identified myself. 'This is Jim Hackett.' He said, 'Is this the Jim Hackett who taped me into the locker?' I didn't hesitate, 'No. I cut you out.'"

When the Harbaugh boys were kids and had the run of the football building, Michigan players often taped Jim and older brother John with what Hackett called a "fence of tape" into the open lockers as a joke.

The ice was broken. Hackett had Harbaugh's attention and got to work. "I said to him, 'Jim, I'm starting down a path here trying to figure out what to do, and you're the first guy I'd like to talk to about this,'" Hackett said. "We didn't talk about the job. We talked about Michigan, philosophically what Michigan needed, and how we both saw it. In a subsequent call, he said, 'You didn't just offer me the job did you?' I told him no. 'I didn't accept, did I?' I said no. He said, 'Good because we're both getting excited here.' We wanted to honor his employment. These talks were just spectacular. It was so easy. It was incredible because of his zest for life and how he sees people and values them. It was really easy. It was a similar philosophy about things. I was surprised actually how aligned we are and still are [considering the] difference in generation. And he was a football coach, and I was a business guy."

But because they were both coached by Schembechler, Hackett said they had the ability to communicate on a different plane. There was an inherent bond, though their playing days were years apart. "He didn't want to sign the agreement until the season was over," Hackett said. "Because of who he played for and I played for, how we were both raised, I just needed to hear him. If you want to tell me you're coming, that's all I need. He said, 'I'm coming.'"

Harbaugh would not make it official until December 28 when the 49ers' season had concluded. He had not even seen a contract from Michigan until after the game and it had been made official he would no longer be coaching the 49ers.

There was a moment of mild panic when Hackett, who had been

faxing contracts with Harbaugh's representation, was flying back to Michigan from California and could not get his computer to work on the plane. Hackett wanted to get his signed offer to Harbaugh, so he used his phone to take a photo and emailed it to the Harbaugh camp.

Harbaugh pulled an upset in NFL circles and signed the agreement with his alma mater on Monday and flew to Ann Arbor the next day for his introductory news conference. Hackett, despite Harbaugh's urging to stay on as Michigan's athletic director, decided to leave U-M 13 months later to become the chairman of Ford Smart Mobility; more recently he became Ford president and CEO. He attends Michigan games when he can and keeps track of what is going on at his alma mater. And he praises Harbaugh for the turnaround. "I don't want to take any credit for it," Hackett said. "I haven't had to coach a down of football. That's where the hard work is. I was committed to the success of it, so I'm proud of that."

1

Just Do It

ON A WARM EVENING IN THE LATE HOURS OF JULY 31, 2016, the crowd of people on State Street in Ann Arbor swelled outside of the M Den, the primary University of Michigan athletics apparel retailer. One eager fan drove north from Columbus, Ohio, to arrive at 8:00 that Sunday morning just for the chance to be first in line.

It was festive. The Michigan Marching Band showed up, as did the dance team. There was a disc jockey, and former players, like Jamie Morris and Marcus Ray, arrived early to sign autographs. The buildup had begun weeks earlier with occasional photo releases of new Nike merchandise, and emotions were bubbling that night as another new era was about to begin.

Nike was coming back in a big way, aligning itself to Michigan athletics with an added touch to the football uniforms. The Jordan Brand and its famed Jumpman logo—forever linked to Michael Jordan and basketball—had made Michigan football the first in its fold.

It felt like another result of what many around Michigan had started calling "The Harbaugh Effect," a Midas touch of sorts for all things football after the hiring in December 2014 of one of its own, former Michigan quarterback Jim Harbaugh. He was a 14-year veteran NFL quarterback, had coached and transformed college programs, most recently Stanford, and had been coach of the San Francisco 49ers, even taking them to the Super Bowl to face off against his brother John's Baltimore Ravens.

Former interim athletic director Jim Hackett, who had done the unthinkable and brought Harbaugh to Michigan after so many NFL pundits had said there was no way that could happen, spent just more than a year on the job and restructured and revitalized the sagging football program, breathing life into its weakened state. Hackett has often compared Harbaugh to the late, great Paul Brown, who Hackett's father had known well, because of their shared nature as innovators in the game of football. And with Harbaugh's encouragement, Hackett negotiated the contract with Nike that electrified a fanbase that had been given its biggest jolt a year earlier by putting Harbaugh at the helm of the football program.

Things evolved and changed pretty quickly after Harbaugh was hired. For the first time in more than five years, according to Hackett, Michigan had a waiting list for season tickets. This was a marked change from the 2014 season when attendance dipped, and there were bargain-basement deals for tickets—unheard of for a program with the biggest football stadium.

It didn't hurt that Michigan State and Ohio State, Michigan's two rivalry games, would be played in Michigan Stadium in 2015, but Harbaugh's hire dramatically affected sales. And Halloween costumes. During that first fall of the Harbaugh Era, countless fans took to Twitter to share photos of themselves dressed as the Michigan coach wearing his standard khakis, blue Michigan sweatshirt, and Block M hat. It's fair to say most didn't don his most unique accessory—black cleats.

Fast forward several months. If anyone wanted signs of a program rebirth, beyond the 10–3 season in Harbaugh's first season in 2015, this was it—thousands of Michigan fans eager to be the first to see the new Nike product and purchase it in a festival-like setting. As the time ticked down to 11:59 PM when the M Den doors would open to the first sales, it felt like New Year's Eve in the heart of summer in southeast Michigan.

A buzz began to build. Desmond Howard, Michigan's 1991 Heisman Trophy winner, was there, along with LaMarr Woodley and former Fab Five member Jimmy King. Store employees suddenly appeared outside the store to pass out specially made pins by Nike for the event. They were rewards for that effort. Some of the pins carried the famous slogan, "Those who stay will be champions," another had a Block M and the Jumpman logo. There was a pin that paid homage to Harbaugh's signature khakis.

As fans were randomly handed pins, they realized there was one of Harbaugh's face in full yelling-at-an-official mode. This became the needle in the haystack they all coveted. "I want a Harbaugh," fans said, as they poked around the pins to see if they could make the rare find. "I want a Harbaugh!"

Not long after, the real deal—Harbaugh—showed up, and fans became fixated on his presence. No one affiliated with the evening's festivities, the four-hour "Welcome Rally" for the Nike launch, knew if he would stop by. There was a chance, but it certainly wasn't planned. Some of his players were there, including top-rated freshman Rashan Gary, but Harbaugh was a surprise.

But here he was inside the store talking to a number of people, including athletic director Warde Manuel. He looked excited about the evening. As the coach emerged from the store, fans pushed against the security ropes to get as close as possible to Harbaugh, who seemed more rock star than football coach that night.

Harbaugh, with some assistance, made his way through the crowd as fans cheered their second-year coach, who had returned to rescue his alma mater's program, which had stumbled for much of the previous decade. Wearing his khakis, a grey Nike hoodie, and his ever-present skinny Block M hat, he worked his way to the stage and took the microphone. "This is Coach Harbaugh here," he said, drawing cheers. "I've lived 52 years, a lot of those years in Ann Arbor, Michigan, and I've never seen anything like this. This is *big time*. The thing that's striking me right now: we aspire to dream big. We aspire to win championships."

The crowd went crazy, drinking in his every word. Dreaming big is important to Harbaugh. He often says, "The message is simple: We want our dreams to be big. We want our goals to be lofty. We want to dream those dreams so much that people would laugh at us. If they're not laughing at us, then we haven't set high enough goals."

With the State Street crowd captivated, Harbaugh gave them one more moment to cherish in his impromptu speech. He wants lofty goals and so he put it out there. But no one laughed. They merely roared louder with approval. "This looks the way it should be when we win a championship," he told them as he gazed at the thousands of fans jamming State Street.

He was drowned by the cheers. A championship. Michigan hasn't had one of those in a long while. Harbaugh got their attention again when he yelled "Go Blue!" and threw his right fist in the air before deciding to lead the crowd in "The Victors." At one point he jumped on a box on the stage while singing and raised both arms in victory a la Rocky.

This is why Jim Harbaugh is in Ann Arbor. He's working to win championships and to restore Michigan to a place of prominence in college football, a place it always has been accustomed to being. Harbaugh understands Michigan's rich history, having been a part of the program as a quarterback under legendary Bo Schembechler and before that as a child playing in the football building with older brother, John, while their beloved father, Jack, worked as an assistant for Schembechler.

Harbaugh understands Schembechler's slogans that have been weaved forever into the fabric of Michigan football: *The Team, the team, the team. Those who stay will be champions.* And he invokes his father's saying frequently, often questioning his players or Michigan fans with, "Who's got it better than us?" pausing before bellowing, "NOOOOObody!"

He is a curious blend of that old-school tradition, wearing the skinny Block M that Schembechler wore, and new-school hip. He's the guy who can appear in a bright yellow sports car in a rap video and later don Woody Hayes-style glasses to wear while coaching. This marriage of Michigan and Nike is what appeals to young, potential recruits. The Jumpman logo on Michigan gear and that affiliation with Michael Jordan greatness? Harbaugh must have been asking himself, *Who's got it better than that?*

There's no doubt he has some quirky traits, and those might also be part of his appeal. He wears his cleats all the time, even occasionally showing up at his Monday night in-season radio show wearing them as he sits down to chat while sipping on a milkshake at The Pizza House before a crowd of fans who are regulars.

Kyle Kalis, who played his final year for Michigan in 2016, told NFL.com it was always amusing to the players that Harbaugh wore cleats. "Two years ago we played Utah in his first game, and it was at Utah," Kalis said. "We took a visit to the Mormon Tabernacle. It was a mile-and-a-half walk, and he made everyone get up early, and we all walked over there. We get inside and we hear this click, clack, click, clack, and Coach Harbaugh's in there with his cleats on. And the Mormon Tabernacle's a pretty nice place, you know, marble floors. All the players are wearing sneakers, and we can't believe Coach Harbaugh's got his cleats on. He's always got those things on."

Harbaugh eats, sleeps, and dreams football. As each season nears, he literally does the latter two. The scenario is always the same—the final drive of the game, and Harbaugh, No. 4, is playing. He never sees how it ends, though. But when he has that dream, which he started having when he was nine years old, he knows the season is about to commence. "I'm always playing in my football dream," he said, "never coaching in my football dream. At the end there's always a final drive that I'm trotting out for, and I always wake up for some reason. I'm waiting for that dream to finish and see how it plays out. Sometimes it's different—like we're ahead—sometimes we're behind, sometimes the score is different, and things happen different to get to that point. [There's] the smell and the feel of running out into the huddle to start the final drive. There's different ways I've gotten there. Sometimes I've started the game, sometimes I come in as the backup. Sometimes I'm young, sometimes I'm like

50, and they signed me just to play that game."

Harbaugh loves big moments, as his dream proves, and this event on August 31, 2016, was nothing short of that. It was the culmination of a series of phone calls and meetings that had begun a year earlier when 1997 Heisman Trophy winner Charles Woodson, who has a personal Jordan Brand contract, texted his friend Michael Jordan about joining forces with Michigan and Harbaugh. It was just a thought, one of those written-on-a-napkin ideas, and Woodson put out the feeler before contacting anyone at Michigan. "That got the ball rolling," Woodson said.

Jordan liked the idea. A lot. So Woodson spoke to Hackett and then Harbaugh to get their blessing and he ran with the idea and followed up with Jordan. For Harbaugh realigning with Nike was important for him from the get-go, particularly for recruiting purposes. And as every coach knows, recruiting is the lifeblood of a program. "Second day on the job I said, 'I really want to be with Nike,'" Harbaugh said.

A month before his first season at Michigan, Harbaugh's phone rang, and it was Jordan. In part because of a poor phone connection and also because he was shocked to be taking a call from Michael Jordan, Harbaugh didn't quite buy it. "My phone rang, a number I didn't know. I said hello and didn't catch the whole name," Harbaugh said. "I said, 'Excuse me, the phone cut out, who is this?' He said, 'This is Michael Jordan.' I said, 'Come on! Come on! Who is it?'

"[He said], 'This is Michael Jordan.' I said, 'The real Michael Jordan?' That's kind of how it went."

A year later, as Harbaugh basked in the frenzy the Nike deal had created and the launch of the Jumpman football uniforms, he recalled that pivotal conversation that had been set in motion by Woodson. "I said, 'You had me at hello,'" Harbaugh said of his phone call with Jordan.

Although the Jumpman logo on a football uniform might have initially been an unusual juxtaposition, it is a union between two legendary brands that appeals to young athletes and recruits and, clearly, legions of Michigan fans who are wearing the Michigan Jordan Brand apparel. "To me, it has nothing to do with basketball," Woodson said of the Jumpman logo. "It's all about Michael Jordan's greatness. Before you look at the championships and the MVPs, what went into Michael? What got him there? That's to me what the Jumpman is about. Yeah, Michael Jordan is the greatest basketball player, and that opinion is shared by a lot of people, myself included. But how did he get there? It's all about the work. How did this university get to where it is now? It didn't just pop up here one day and all of a sudden it's one of the greatest universities we know. There's a lot that went into it, and to me, that's what the Jumpman is all about. It's about that journey to get to that point where somebody can revere you as the greatest of all time."

Harbaugh saw that link—Michigan and Jordan—immediately and knew what it could mean, not just to consumers and not just to recruits. Harbaugh gravitates toward those who are the best in their professions. By associating with greatness, you can become great and you learn. Every day is an education, and Harbaugh appreciates the lessons he can take from those who have achieved in whatever field.

This is not to say he looks down at the rest. Instead, he pulls from his vast connections he has developed over the years to enhance his team—in this case the University of Michigan and its football program. "As Jack Harbaugh said, 'You are with whom you associate,'" Harbaugh said. "To be associated with greatness and to think about having Michael Jordan sharing a sideline with us...to have that iconic logo sharing the uniform, we're very, very proud of that."

That much was clear as he stood on that stage on State Street nearing midnight with throngs of fans eagerly awaiting the start of another season full of promise.

2

The Harbaugh Boys

B Y THE SUMMER AFTER JIM HARBAUGH'S FIRST SEASON at Michigan, he had, as many people described, won the offseason. He was in the college football news constantly after the Wolverines had won the New Year's Day bowl game against Florida. Isn't this what Michigan fans wanted when Harbaugh was given the keys to the program? Didn't they want Michigan to be back with the bar set high for Big Ten titles and the promise of national playoff appearances?

With Harbaugh, Michigan fans knew they had a game-changer. What they probably didn't realize right off the bat is he was determined to change the game off the field as well.

He had already caused upheaval the previous summer with the "Summer Swarm Tour" of satellite camps as he and his staff visited high schools across the country to spread the game of football and the Michigan football brand. And maybe, just maybe, they were able to get in front of a few recruits, particularly in the fertile recruiting areas of Florida, Alabama, Texas, and California.

But by the summer of 2016, he had not only decided to expand his massive satellite tour to include stops in Hawaii, American Samoa, and Australia, seemingly thumbing his nose at a collection of peeved Division I coaches, but he also pushed new buttons when he did the unthinkable and took his team to IMG Academy in Bradenton, Florida, over spring break as part of spring practice. Michigan had four practices there, and the players were given an opportunity for some fun in the sun. Spring football trips had been anything but the norm for football programs across the country. Baseball, softball, tennis, golf, and basketball teams are among scholarship sports that will take preseason trips for practice, but it was unheard of for football.

While Harbaugh was praised by the Michigan faithful, he drew criticism from many college football circles, primarily rival conference commissioners who sought to cancel the summer camps and criticized the spring break trip as infringing on the student-athletes' free time. He deftly used social media—he has more than a million followers on Twitter—to take less-than-subtle digs at rival coaches. Though not referring to them by name, his points were always clear and stinging.

Coaches were clearly divided on the satellite camp front. Many said their time is already consumed by football, and spending more time away from home just didn't work. Others, thinking along the lines of Harbaugh, understood its value as a recruiting tool and a way to expose high school players to a number of different schools. Other programs had taken part in those types of camps over the years, but the expanded reach of Michigan's efforts was unequalled.

Michigan defensive line coach Greg Mattison could see why competing coaches didn't like this Harbaugh move. Coaches have so little time off these days, and working that amount of camps would erase their dwindling free time. But in part what the camps do is put Michigan in front of players that maybe Michigan would never see or otherwise have a chance to woo.

Conversely, many players who hadn't thought about Michigan would get a chance to at least consider the Wolverines. And, really, the majority attending the camp might have Division I aspirations but not be destined for, say, Michigan. They might get on the radar of other staffs working the camps, so in Harbaugh's mind, this was a win-win.

Considering his belief—shared by his father and brother—that the game is under attack, Harbaugh would call it the most fun he had, spreading the Gospel of Football. There, he could be out in the sweltering heat, wearing khakis, his blue sweatshirt, and a jersey of someone famous from the area while coaching young boys how to play—and love—football. "They are tremendous," Mattison said of the camps. "You may not get a player out of them, you may get one or two, you may get a whole bunch, but what better thing is there for football than to take the Michigan football staff to a part of the country, coach young men—it's not expensive—let them get better at football, they get to know what we are, and then get in a plane or get in a car and get to the next place? Isn't that what coaches are supposed to do, try to help guys get better? That's what Jim's doing. Yeah, you might have contact with a young man at that camp who becomes a player, or he might like the coaching staff. He's never going to get to Michigan. A kid from Dallas is not going to get on a plane and fly here...if it's not a paid visit."

If it wasn't Harbaugh mixing it up by challenging NCAA rules and their loopholes, he made news by staging a Signing Day gala called "Signing of the Stars" on campus at Hill Auditorium in February. Lines of fans stretched outside the auditorium to get a seat to watch the spectacle, featuring all of Michigan's new recruits on the first day of the National Signing Period and a diverse group of celebrities like Tom Brady, Derek Jeter, and Ric Flair.

Harbaugh also made news in his second season of revitalizing Michigan by visiting the White House and being a guest at a State of the Union address. He appeared in a rap video; coached first base in a spring training game; drew attention for taking his baseball glove to a World Series game; reintroduced the college world to his creation, Freddy P. Soft; played golf in a Pro-Am; messed around playing some drums on stage before a Bruce Springsteen concert; called rival coaches who he believed were negatively recruiting against him, "Jive Turkeys;" and he waxed poetic about how much he respects the animated character, SpongeBob.

He is a different guy, a move-the-needle guy. Some argue he's calculated. Some say he's as authentic as they come. He probably falls somewhere in between.

But whatever he is, he's been sure to be everywhere—from

causing a stir with sleepovers at some homes of recruits, showing up at 12:01 AM to try to pack in as much as possible in the 24 hours he's allowed to visit—to captivating everyone with his attempt to climb a tree while playing with the younger siblings of another recruit.

While the sleepovers were wildly mocked nationally, Harbaugh saw it as a unique and creative opportunity to legally take advantage of the rules. "When I saw it, I thought it was genius because it's not a show," Mattison said. "It truly isn't a show. We went to a home, and he was going to do a sleepover. We were sitting in the living room, and he goes, 'Okay, I'm doing this [since] I don't ever have enough time to be with the family. We're going to talk about football, we're going to talk about whatever, talk about life. I'm going to sleep here on the couch, and in the morning, we're going to get up and go to school.' They get to see who the head coach is other than a salesman."

In this social media era, almost every move he makes, like sleepovers at the homes of recruits, is documented and dissected, criticized and lauded. And more often than not, it leads to a headline and maybe even debate on local and national radio sports talk shows. For a storied program that seemed to have lost its way, seeing Michigan back in the news on whatever front has been a positive for most former players.

During the summer of 2016, Charles Woodson, Michigan's 1997 Heisman Trophy winner, was asked if he was surprised how much Harbaugh is in the news. "I don't know if I'm shocked," Woodson said. "But it's almost overwhelming. To me, every time you look on the TV or you look at a tweet or something on social media, somewhere, Jim Harbaugh's name is a part of it. What that means for us—Michigan is a part of it, too. For the guys who played here, the guys who are here, they're getting a lot of attention. The great part about that, you have an opportunity to perform with all eyes on you. That can be extra pressure depending on how you look at it, or you can embrace it and show people about the work you put into it day in and day out, and your coach is out there speaking on your behalf because your coach believes in you. Am I surprised? Maybe, maybe not. But I'm happy. This is what a majority of people wanted, and we got it."

When Harbaugh was hired at the end of 2014 to coach his alma mater and resuscitate the program, a number of his former Michigan teammates trumpeted his return. "Unequivocally, I would play with him again," John Kolesar, a former UM receiver who caught passes from Harbaugh, said. "I would want to coach with him and I would want my son to play for him. I've seen him work, I've seen him sacrifice, and I've seen him want to be better and want great things for himself. He instilled an innate confidence that emanated from him and was absorbed in the huddle by his teammates. He's been bred for this."

Another teammate, Derrick Walker, called Harbaugh "a winner" and a guy who would "bring instant credibility." "He brings a winning culture," Walker said. Jamie Morris, a Michigan fixture and former running back, also played with Harbaugh. "If Jimmy said we were going to win, we were going to win," he said. "That's how he was."

During the summer of 2016, a coffee table book Harbaugh co-authored featuring the black-and-white photos of Pulitzer-prize winning photographer David Turnley, a Michigan alum back at the school teaching, was published. Turnley chronicled the 2015 season in this book, for which Harbaugh wrote what essentially is his 16-page treatise on coaching and being part of a team. The first two words of his treatise is the name of Bo Schembechler, Harbaugh's college coach and most important mentor. "I first fell in love with the University of Michigan as a child, when my father was an assistant coach, and that love has only grown over time," Harbaugh wrote. "But that alone would not help us achieve our goals."

He then shared his thoughts on the Michigan program being built on 15 principles. Among them were: attitude, enthusiasm, hard work, decision-making, problem-solving, being coachable, having discipline, and his 15th principle, "Who's got it better than us?"

It is a motto that his father, Jack, began in their household as Jim, his older brother, John, and younger sister, Joani, grew up. "Each time I heard the chant, 'Who's got it better than us?' and the response, 'Noooooooooboody!' we are all saying, 'I believe in you and I'm hearing that you believe in me,'" Harbaugh wrote. "And that brings a smile to my face. Try it, see how it works."

Michigan fans, college football fans have an idea who Jim Harbaugh is. He was the coach hired to return Michigan to a lofty perch in the game, he wears khakis and a blue Michigan sweatshirt even when it's blazing hot, he likes Twitter, he likes pushing the envelope, and he loves to compete. A *Vanity Fair* story last spring about the Rolling Stones' Mick Jagger could have been describing Harbaugh. "One in a million, a freak of nature," the story read. "Can't be copied, only enjoyed...You want to peg him and walk away but can't."

Harbaugh, in the simplest of terms, is the ultimate competitor. But he is a complex personality. Some might also describe him as a freak of nature who restlessly seeks the next challenge and, more importantly, the next victory. "We used to play this game called chicken," John Harbaugh, who coaches the Baltimore Ravens, said, as he animatedly described a scene involving the two young Harbaugh brothers. "We'd line up as far apart as we could and zing balls at each other and take a step closer for every catch until finally somebody cracked."

John Harbaugh beamed and could barely hide his enthusiasm as he shared the memory. Who usually was the first to crack? "I don't think it was me," he said while Jim Harbaugh stood next to him, not saying a word. "I think I won most of them, but he'd say the opposite." John Harbaugh laughed easily. "We were always bruised."

The brothers, 15 months apart, have always been competitive. John knew Jim was a good athlete from an early age. "Maybe as soon as I can remember," John said. "The thing about Jim, he was always big. I was born, and then he caught up. I'd get a growth spurt, and then he would catch up and pass me until he got to be 6'3" and when he became strapping twisted blue steel."

John smiled again, amused at his description, the same one Bo Schembechler often used to describe himself—twisted blue steel. "I tell the story sometimes," John said. "We took a vacation, I was 26, 27, Jim had been in the NFL three, four years, and we took the family vacation to Amelia Island. Little did I know there was a reason he brought us there. We get out on the beach. Maybe the last fight, maybe I had gotten the upper hand. Maybe something was bothering him. We get in a wrestling match on the beach, and next thing I know, he takes me down—under the water. I thought, 'Okay, he took me down, I'll pop back up, we're having fun right?' I'm still under the water and I'm still under the water and I get this feeling like, 'I don't think he's gonna let me up right away. Is this the moment? Is this what it's all come to? Has he finally snapped? Has he finally gone over the edge? Is this going to be the end?' He finally let me up and looked at me like, 'Does that settle it once and for all?' That would be the way I'd go down."

Jim stood there, alongside their father, Jack, and listened without interjecting, without changing his facial expression. He can maintain that look for a long time, emotionless, expressionless. Did he remember that scene? "I do. I was just waiting for it, waiting for it," Jim said looking at John. "Every time you tell that story, you really get into it. It's very theatrical, it's very self-deprecating because," and at this point he used a humorous, slightly mocking voice, "I've got you under the water. This is the end. This was the final confrontation. Every time that story has ever been told, it leads to…"

"That's not true," John said jumping in.

"At the Super Bowl, you had me under the water," Jim said.

And with a simple thank you from John, the verbal game of chicken ended, but no one was bruised.

Jack Harbaugh has said that he wishes he could have come up coaching with both of his sons because he would have learned so much. Although his sons are cut from the same competitive cloth, they are different. Maybe that's because John is in the NFL, and Jim has returned to college. Jim has made so much noise since his arrival at Michigan in part because the college version of the game lends itself to a rah-rah personality. He can be Jim vs. the Officials, or Jim vs. the NCAA, or Jim vs. the Southeastern Conference because college football sets itself up for those inner battles.

Whatever it is, not only have Michigan fans relished seeing their coaching mixing it up and garnering headlines, but his brother has enjoyed it, as well. "I love it," John said. "It's my No. 1 thing that I pull up because there's something new there every day. It's great entertainment. It's been fun to watch. It's supposed to be fun. It's sports."

Like Woodson, John Harbaugh hasn't been shocked by anything he's seen from his brother. "It doesn't surprise me," John said. "I'm just impressed with the degree he's been able to create. It is inspiring. We both believe the same thing. I see how he hasn't been afraid, and he's unapologetic, doing things right, nothing to apologize for. It motivates me to want to create and find ways people haven't thought about. It is as Admiral Gates said: 'If you haven't made any enemies, you haven't done anything in life.' The competitors are usually mad at you. He's enjoying it here, I know that."

John laughed when asked if his brother had always had "the Look," that intense staring shark-like gaze while his mouth is slightly agape. It is an intimidating look, typically making the recipient uneasy. "You mean this," John said, laughing, as he pushed his face forward into the face of a reporter and stared. "Don't take it personally."

"No, no, don't take it personally," Jim, who had witnessed the scene, said. "I'm just thinking."

When NFL pundits were insisting Harbaugh would never leave the NFL, not even for Michigan, they often cited his wife, Sarah, as someone who would never move to the Midwest. Somehow she had been labeled a Californian, even though, as she later pointed out, she's from Kansas City and as Midwest as you could possibly be. So why would the thought of living in the Midwest repel her?

She has seen her young children thrive in Ann Arbor, attending the schools her husband attended and visiting the Michigan football building just as he and John and Joani did as kids. "They love being able to go to work with Jim at the football office and going to the games," Sarah said.

While her husband is constantly asked for photographs or autographs, Sarah peels off to the side, eager to step out of that spotlight. She understands Michigan's connection to her husband and vice versa, but it is more different than she could have imagined. "It's great in the sense there's so much love for Michigan football. There always has been, but I wasn't expecting the abundance," Sarah said. "Every place we've been, people have loved the team or the coach, but here there's an all-around love for the University of Michigan. Every day I understand more and more why there are 500,000 alums and every time I run into a Michigan alum I've never heard a negative story."

She does know there are negative things said about her husband and negative stories written. She avoids listening to radio shows and reading much that's out there about Michigan football. "He's so misunderstood by so many people, and I'd want to call in to defend him," she said. "It makes me angry because I can't defend him."

Sarah Harbaugh doesn't focus much on the negative. She knows it's out there, but she also knows what her husband is trying to accomplish at his alma mater. He has his parents, Jack and Jackie, in Ann Arbor now, living close by. Jack is at Schembechler Hall almost daily. He's invigorated by being back at Michigan and he's in the building, at practices, serving as a sounding board for his son. It's idyllic, really, and has come full circle in a sense. "I'm so happy to be back and happy for the future," Sarah said. "I hope it's a long future here."

3

Fun in the Sun

THE 2016 NATIONAL CHAMPIONSHIP GAME WASN'T cold yet, and already the way, way, way too early four-team national playoff team projections were being published by several national pundits in early January. Surprisingly, Michigan, which blistered Florida in a New Year's Day bowl game, was listed among the four teams. Entering their second season under Jim Harbaugh; with a new quarterback to break in; a new defensive coordinator in Don Brown, whom the players called Dr. Blitz and admiringly spoke of his mustache; and despite several unknowns; the Wolverines were among those at the top of the heap.

Brown had coached Boston College to the nation's No. 1 defense in 2015 and he inherited a veteran defense at Michigan with which to work, not to mention a prized athlete in Jabrill Peppers, who could pretty much play anywhere needed, including on offense and special teams. The bowl victory did wonders for the Wolverines' confidence. A year after missing out on a bowl, they went from 5–7 B.H. (before Harbaugh) to 10–3 under Harbaugh's watch. "That Florida game was important," tight end Jake Butt said. "It set the bar for our whole entire offseason. We had their number that day, and the one thing we talked about in our spring football meetings was raising the bar. We raised the bar to play Florida. That's now ground zero. Now we've got to raise the bar a couple more levels in the spring."

Harbaugh raised the bar that spring—both for his players and for college football.

He did what no one else had done in his sport and packed up the team during the university's spring break and headed to Florida. There, at the IMG Academy in Bradenton, south of Tampa and not far from the coast and the beaches, the team would get in four practices and some fun time.

The idea was not a new one, just new for college football. Many college teams head to warm weather to prepare for their seasons, but no one takes a football team off campus. Except Harbaugh. "He's one of a kind," Butt said. "He thinks out of the box. I think that's big. I may not, and a lot of us probably don't understand the reason behind a lot of the things he does, but I can assure you there's a reason behind everything he does. He has a plan for everything. He's doing most of the things for the betterment of our team and our program."

Yeah, well, that wasn't flying with the commissioners of the Atlantic Coast Conference and the Southeastern Conference. John Swofford, the ACC commissioner, agreed with Butt's sentiment that Harbaugh was thinking outside the box, but that's about all he would agree with.

During an interview on Sirius XM College Sports, he said the plan to take the Wolverines off-site for a week of practice during spring break would be addressed at the NCAA level because of time demand issues. That is an issue that had become a top priority for the NCAA. He echoed SEC commissioner Greg Sankey's earlier comments that Harbaugh's plan was being negligent to student-athletes. "It is creative," Swofford told the show. "It's kind of like we're going to take you on vacation, but you've got to practice while we're on vacation…it's a huge intrusion on a college student's life and taking his ability to have a break out of his hands. I guess it depends on how you look at it."

Sankey said the SEC had asked the NCAA to prevent football programs from taking a trip like Harbaugh had planned. Michigan would leave Ann Arbor on February 28, return on March 5, have four practices in Florida, enjoy two outings to the beach, and play Putt-Putt, among other non-football-related activities.

Because of its 140-character limit, Harbaugh has identified

Twitter as a short and sweet way to share his responses or messages. After Sankey had made his comments, Harbaugh seemed to take a shot at Sankey on Twitter with the post: "Question of the day: Does anyone find whining to be attractive? Just curious." Sankey responded to the tweet in an Alabama-based newspaper. "I'm not going to reduce what is an important conversation to some childhood use of Twitter," Sankey said. "This is an important issue."

It was like watching a verbal boxing match without the sweat and blood but with the fun of watching a zinger land. Swofford would not be drawn into the Harbaugh-Sankey exchange, but he was asked if Harbaugh's idea is a "brilliant" move or whether it needs to be addressed. "It's an issue we need to address," he said. "It's certainly out-of-the-box thinking and creative thinking, but on the other hand, to me, and this is just one man's opinion, it seems a bit in contrast to the overall thinking that we're all trying to put into time demands for student-athletes and giving our athletes more time to have to themselves to be more a part of a college experience and be more a part of college life, and to require a practice during an offseason practice period during an academic spring break seems to me to be at odds with the bigger picture of what we're trying to do in terms of time demands on our athletes."

Harbaugh had said part of the reason he wanted to practice during spring break was to leave the players two weeks during finals or "discretionary weeks" for them to focus on their academics. He said it also offered a trip for those who can't afford to take a spring break trip.

And not lost in all of this is that IMG Academy has a football team with some of the nation's most sought-after recruits. They would be able to drop by the final practice, and high school coaches from across Florida could visit practice at any time.

While commissioners and national columnists debated this latest Harbaugh twist, Butt sort of became the unofficial spokesman for the team while maybe even auditioning for a future role with the Florida Chamber of Commerce. "We're away, we're down here in Florida, beautiful territory, sunshine, not too hot, nice breeze, eating great food with our brothers," Butt said. "I don't have anything negative to say about it. More teams should do it."

Butt has never been afraid to share his opinions on players' rights and he certainly always publicly supported his coaches and teammates. He could not stop sharing what a great idea it was to be away for a week and practicing in the heat. "No one asked us about it," Butt said. "If you would have asked me, I would have backed [Harbaugh] up right away. And I really would encourage it for a lot of other people. This first week of spring ball, it's tough. You're learning new plays, you're building that callus where you're really sore. You're doing these four-hour practices. We don't have to worry about these with classes now. All we have to worry about is football and [then] we're out on the beach relaxing. It's unbelievable because not everybody on our team is going to get a spring break, to get away or anything like that."

Harbaugh brought those aforementioned four-hour practices to Michigan in spring of 2015. The players looked at the schedule and thought it was a typo. Certainly it was a joke. *Four hours of practice?* No one practices four hours. But Harbaugh's feeling was it's always better to have what he calls "class on grass" to speed up the learning curve.

He also knew what he was inheriting. The personnel was fine, but some players admitted to the program having had more of a "country club" feel, and they were, frankly, soft. That showed toward the end of games in 2014. The team wasn't finishing, and something was lacking. "We were struggling with toughness our first few years," Butt said of the seasons of which he was a part with then-coach Brady Hoke before Harbaugh arrived. "It was something down the stretch of games when your backs were against the wall. We struggled and we lost a lot of games. Coach Harbaugh identified this and he made the changes necessary, and it paid off for us last year."

In Florida the coaches were working six hours a day. The younger players came out earlier, then the entire team overlapped, and then the older players received focused practice time, so that it worked out to four hours for each group.

By Year Two the players had bought in. They had seen the results in that first season and knew this was the way to build toward that four-team national playoff, for which they had been projected. "He doesn't take any days off," Butt said referring to Harbaugh. "He doesn't ask any of us to do anything that he's not willing to do himself. He forces us to be tough. When you're out there practicing four hours, smashing into each other, you don't have any choice but to be tough. He's probably the most competitive person I have ever met and probably will ever meet. That being said, I try to match that competitiveness, for sure. When you're out there for four hours, you're sweating. He's got us in the indoor facility [in Ann Arbor], the heat turned up. Our one offense against our one defense. You have no choice but to be competitive."

Michigan beat writers arrived in Florida, as did several national media members. After all, this was a national story, considering all the noise surrounding the spring break trip Harbaugh orchestrated that week. Harbaugh never opens practices to media, including in the spring, preseason, and season. Imagine the surprise when reporters received a mass text message saying to arrive early at IMG for open access.

This was shocking but not really. Harbaugh proved in 2015 he knew how to win the offseason, and here was an opportunity to hold court while throwing a few bones to reporters. "We're just out here to get better every day and play football," he told a group after the first day of practice in sunny Florida. "You can only get better at football by playing football."

That is a frequent Harbaughism.

Legendary Dick Vitale, who lives in the area, dropped by practice wearing a Michigan hat. A smattering of high school coaches also lined the sidelines to observe. "I always felt like the first day of spring practice and the first day of fall camp, those were my two favorite days of the year," Harbaugh said. "It's like the New Year."

Naturally, he was asked what he thought of the criticism and various rivals thinking this was an issue. "I don't know why," he said. "Our tennis team is going to be hitting balls here this week."

Drama aside, Michigan really was there to focus on improvement. It was also time for the new coordinator, Brown, to get to know his defensive players and vice versa. Brown also let everyone in on a little secret—he was moving standout Peppers, who the season before was named the Big Ten's Freshman of the Year, from safety to a hybrid linebacker role. Peppers had played on offense and returned kicks the previous year, but Brown wanted to expand and diversify his contributions on defense in his attacking, blitz-heavy defense. "We've got to give this guy a bunch of jobs," Brown said of Peppers. "He's a dynamic athlete, and we'll keep him around the line of scrimmage and let him do a bunch of stuff, whether it's cover, whether it's in certain personnel groups to play linebacker."

Harbaugh, who had hired Brown two months earlier without ever meeting him in person, gave his stamp of approval. He said he could not wait to see how Peppers would adapt to and embrace this role. "He plays at an athletic level that is so very, very high," Harbaugh said. "We saw what he can do last year in terms of picking up a new position. It's seamless for him. He's very intelligent, is so competitive, he's got it all. Athletic ability and awareness, you would say those are the two most important things after sheer competitiveness. He's got all those three things at the highest level."

Meanwhile, Michigan had to move on from Jake Rudock, the graduate transfer quarterback from Iowa who led the Wolverines the previous year, and were entrenched in a quarterback competition involving Wilton Speight, Rudock's backup the year before; Shane Morris; and John O'Korn.

By Thursday, Harbaugh, who never opted for lightweight

clothing during practice despite the warm temperatures, wore his khakis-and-Michigan-sweatshirt uniform and was in a buoyant mood for the Wolverines' third practice. During a practice-free day the day before, Harbaugh coached three innings at first base for the Detroit Tigers in a spring training game against the Pittsburgh Pirates. One of his first loves was baseball, and he dreamed of being a major leaguer, so being around baseball is always a mood booster for him.

But during that third practice in Florida, he was in such a bright mood that he at one point sidled up to a group of reporters and joked that their arrival to practice had been getting later and later each day. Maybe he knew he was going to stir things up on Twitter later that day. Shortly after that practice concluded, Harbaugh took to Twitter to take a jab at Tennessee coach Butch Jones, who joined in late on what had been a humorous Twitter post from Arkansas coach Bret Bielema directed at Harbaugh.

The day before, Bielema decided to have some fun. He tweeted: "After early meetings & lift tomorrow with our players. Thinking about heading to watch an open practice tomorrow at IMG with the staff." Then Michigan State coach Mark Dantonio retweeted Bielema and added a note: "Want to do lunch?"

Harbaugh went Twitter quiet.

Bielema posted a tweet Thursday morning, saying he found out from the NCAA office he couldn't go to the IMG open practice even if he really wanted to because it's a quiet period in recruiting. But then Jones decided to tack on a tweet to Bielema and Dantonio that day: "Mind if I join you guys for lunch?"

The gloves were off.

Harbaugh had used Twitter to extend birthday wishes, engage with a few celebrities like Judge Judy, and to subtweet with the best of them. His point was more direct, though in his response to Jones, whom he didn't refer to by name. "Suggestion to my Rocky Top colleague, rather than lunch in Florida you might spend your time and focus attending to your present team," Harbaugh wrote, not referring to Jones by name.

Ouch.

The previous week, just before Michigan departed for Florida, Jones offered 20 IMG Academy players scholarships to Tennessee. But surely Harbaugh was referencing the fact Jones and Tennessee were embroiled in a bigger issue. The UT athletic department recently has come under scrutiny for a Title IX lawsuit filed against the school. Jones also was facing allegations he called a player a "traitor" for helping a woman who said she was sexually assaulted by two Tennessee teammates. In the lawsuit eight women accused Tennessee of having a "hostile sexual environment."

After the final practice Friday, which was open to the public and recruits and drew several thousand, Harbaugh, who had made it perfectly clear he didn't care what people were saying about this trip, was asked about the chatter on Twitter from rival coaches. "It's been a wide range," Harbaugh said. "I think my favorite one so far is the comment that this is a circus, like a big circus. They also referenced [Signing Day's] Signing of the Stars. I mean, what a circus. As a youngster I remember the circus coming to town. I remember that, looking forward to it, saving my pennies up and dollars up because the circus was coming to town and couldn't wait. And every circus I ever went to, I always left feeling really great about it, and it was a lot of fun. That's the way I feel about this. It was much-anticipated and it was a heck of a lot of fun."

The players had been consistent in their comments during the week in Florida, saying they had a great time making beach visits, playing ping-pong, and bonding as teammates while getting in four practices.

They feel like Harbaugh is on the cutting edge in terms of outside-the-box thinking and drumming up discussion and all the criticism and praise that goes with it. Tailback Drake Johnson briefly impersonated Harbaugh after that final practice, stretching his arms wide as Harbaugh does when he speaks to them. He told them that no other football team was taking a trip like this. "And that's really how we feel," Johnson said. "No one else is doing what we're doing, and that makes it something special. You always want to be innovative. Anytime you do something special, you do something new, it's going to be memorable, it's going to have that kind of sentiment to it, so I really think by doing this he's created a special bond for our team and for Michigan."

Harbaugh stood up for himself and for the trip. Earlier in the week he had referenced the movie, *Remember the Titans*, which told the story of a high school team in Virginia and its coach who had to shape his football team after two racially segregated schools combined. Emotions were high, and he took the team away from the school to have a preseason camp and to create team bonding.

The Wolverines watched that film during the spring break trip. "You know my feelings on it," he said when asked again about the criticism. "The arguments don't hold water, and this is a really good thing. It's a great thing for everybody involved. I would recommend this to other football programs. I'd recommend it to us to do it again. There were no negatives. There were all positives. The feedback's been really good. The morale's been very, very high. The development's been very good—team development, football development—but also I think it's been real good for guys getting to know each other better. Guys who don't know somebody as well got a real opportunity. There were 19 different meals, sitting down and having a conversation. That was good, watched it all week multiple times. I think they had a lot of fun and I think they worked extremely hard. I thought it was very beneficial for us."

He said his coaches and staff "feel like innovators" because of the plan to take spring practice on the road, but then they laughingly scaled back. He explained that in 1938 the Cornell swim coach took his team to Florida during spring break and created the concept. "Maybe we're giving ourselves a little too much credit on the innovation part," Harbaugh said, laughing. "I did some research on this. This wasn't just a spur-of-the-moment decision. Maybe it's not as innovative as I might have given us credit for."

Bottom line, the purpose of the trip was not to stir up headlines but to prepare for the upcoming season. That's what spring is about. It gives younger players a chance to get reps and gives older players a chance to polish technique and improve. After the final Florida practice, Harbaugh was satisfied that his team was progressing in Year Two just as he had hoped. "We're a team that's better athletically than we were this time last year," he said. "Our awareness is better, and when you have better awareness of what you're doing, you can bring out some of those athletic traits. I'm pleased we're further along that way."

The players said the spring trip went a long way to drawing the team closer. They were already on a high coming off the Citrus Bowl and they continued feeling high-spirited as spring practice concluded with the game. For the first time in years, the Wolverines were carrying themselves with a confidence and swagger. They were surprisingly candid after the spring game about what they expected from the upcoming season. "I truly believe it when I say it: we're up there with some of the best teams in the country and we can compete with anybody in the country this year," Butt said. "I truly believe that, not only because we've got talent at every position, but because we've got guys who are coming back...everyone is competitive and giving it their all every single play. We've got great leadership from the coaching staff and the players all the way down, and I think that will help us."

There, he said it. A bold statement, nothing anyone had heard from a Michigan player in a long, long time. Michigan, they were starting to feel, could be a national contender just as many of the prognosticators said at the start of the year. "That is how we feel," Peppers said. "We've been there. We were 5–7 the year before last year. We bought in. We put the work in. We've seen that if you put the work in, you can bring that [result] back out. That was an eye-opener for a lot of guys who were kind of questioning the regimen. If you buy in and put the work in, things will work themselves out."

4

Youthful Exuberance

I F JIM HARBAUGH IS ANYTHING, HE IS YOUNG AT HEART. There are plenty of examples from throwing with the quarterbacks before every game, to climbing trees on recruiting trips, to being awestruck when meeting a childhood idol, to getting downright giddy when talking about baseball. Being a father holds a special place in his heart. The day before Father's Day in 2016, he paid the ultimate tribute to parenthood. "There's nothing I'd rather be defined as than as a dad," he said. "People define us men in a lot of ways—a doctor, a lawyer, a dentist, a construction worker, teacher, a coach, but being called a dad is the defining moment."

A day after Father's Day, he informed campers that he was going to be a father again. He and wife, Sarah, would have their fourth child, a son, John, to join Addison, Katherine, and Jack. He has three children—Jay, a Michigan assistant coach, James Jr., a student at Michigan, and Grace—from a previous marriage. In true Harbaugh fashion, he told the campers that he and Sarah planned to attack "the pregnancy with an enthusiasm unknown to mankind."

Further proof of his youthful approach was the release in late summer of video featuring Harbaugh with the rapper, Bailey. Five years earlier Bailey wrote a song about the San Francisco 49ers using Harbaugh's—well, Jack Harbaugh's slogan that Jim has adopted: "Who's got it better than us?" It was catchy and highlighted 49ers history and its team at the time.

With Harbaugh at Ann Arbor, Bailey, who is from the Bay Area, revamped the rap and made it Michigan and Harbaugh-centric with Harbaugh in the video belting out the familiar refrain, "Who's got it better than us?" The video opens, panning the inside of Michigan Stadium and the field, and the first words you hear are Harbaugh yelling "Who's Got it Better than Us?" Eventually, you see Bailey walking by all things Michigan football-related and appearing inside the Wolverines' Glick Fieldhouse with Harbaugh. There's a bright yellow Corvette in which Harbaugh, clad in his khakis-long-sleeved shirt-and-hat uniform, sat while bobbing his head to the music.

The lyrics talk about Michigan, of course, Bo, Tom Brady, and Charles Woodson, and the video scans images from the spring game. "I've got one question. Tell 'em, Harbaugh," Bailey says to Harbaugh, who delivers the refrain one more time.

And there's then-52-year-old Jim Harbaugh in the 'Vette, clearly into the music and delivering the refrain with close-ups of him bellowing the words throughout the video. That rap video appearance fit right in with all of the other Harbaughisms that appeal to fans and recruits because it's just a little bit quirky, a little bit endearing, and a lot relatable to young recruits and players.

During the Big Ten Media Days in Chicago that July, he first had to clear up the important subject of why he was wearing his Michigan ball cap with this suit. All of the other coaches were wearing suits. No hats. Hats with suits are usually reserved for the day you're announced as the new head coach. Not so in Harbaugh's world. "I haven't had a hair cut in about five weeks. I do have hair," Harbaugh said, doffing his cap while talking to reporters. "I wear suits and ties when I go to a wedding, and they say you have to wear them for this, but I felt more comfortable with the hat. And I like the skinny M."

Harbaugh then detailed more important things. No, not his 2016 team. That could wait. He was asked about his rap video appearance and he revealed he had a hand in the writing of the rap. That's a little bit of a stretch. Harbaugh had not turned songwriter, but he very proudly announced he added one line to the rap: "Roughest team in the B-I-G."

He was asked why he participated in the rap and the video. "Why not?" Harbaugh said. "My default answer is yes. The feedback has been great. We did not embarrass ourselves. It's a respectable song and video. I've gotten multiple texts, comments, phone calls from people who really like it. All the cool people like it. Some uptight people don't, but they're very few."

All-American cornerback Jourdan Lewis laughed about the video and really wouldn't share specifics of his opinion of the rap, but he chalked it up to Harbaugh being Harbaugh. "I mean, that's out of his element," Lewis said. "It's cool that he tried that. I'm kind of glad he's trying different things. He's not afraid to go out there and try new things. He's just being himself. That's him."

Media days are just what they sound like—a few days in Chicago for media to hear all of the Big Ten coaches discuss their programs and to speak to a few players from each school about their goals and hopes for the upcoming season. Ohio State's Urban Meyer spoke about losing so many players to the NFL, having 44 players who had not taken a collegiate snap and yet he felt great about the talent on this team and its prospects. D.J. Durkin, who had been Michigan's defensive coordinator in 2015, discussed becoming a head coach for the first time and leading Maryland. Michigan State's Mark Dantonio told of the youth on the team that had experienced so many of the highs, but they had to understand that nothing is a given.

Harbaugh immediately downplayed his big offseason, the headlines, the tweets, all of that, when it was pointed out that it had been an entertaining offseason. "I don't know that it has," Harbaugh said in a way that made clear no one would convince him otherwise. "I don't know how entertaining it's really been."

Lewis, Jake Butt, and Amara Darboh were Michigan's player representatives, and Harbaugh raved about each as well as versatile Jabrill Peppers. Butt was the Big Ten's Tight End of the Year the previous season and a Mackey Award finalist who opted to forego leaving early for the NFL to savor another season of college football with his teammates. The same went for Lewis. The All-American and Detroit native, Lewis, had evolved into one of the best cover corners in the country and he, too, flirted with the idea of an early departure to the NFL. Darboh had been overshadowed a bit at the end of 2015 by receiver Jehu Chesson, but after Chesson was injured in the bowl game, Darboh re-emerged as the top receiver on the team.

Harbaugh giddily shared his impressions with the gathered media. "Jake Butt is one of the most gung ho players I've ever been around," Harbaugh said, "can sit through a two-and-a-half-hour, three-hour meeting and be interactive, be on the edge of his seat, walk out of that meeting with a bounce in his step, and put his football gear on, hair on the back of his neck is standing up, excited to get out on the field, and he practices, and whether he's going out to hit his sled or rattle somebody's fillings, just excited about doing that as he is as running a post route or corner route and catching a ball. [He] does all those things equally well as a route runner, as a blocker, as a teammate, and as a guy with some pizzazz. He's gung ho and enjoys the struggle of football, really enjoy him as one of our top players."

He described Lewis as a player who never takes a play off, a quality Harbaugh relishes. "He doesn't diminish his effort at any time," Harbaugh said. "He's an ascending player, improving player. And when he started to get the recognition of being a really good player, All-American, All-Big Ten, interceptions, and acclaim, when he started getting the acclaim, he didn't change a bit. He went through the entire spring practice wanting to get better, wanting to improve every single day...And he's a likable guy. He's respected by everybody on the team, but he also has the personality of being very competitive but being very likable with his teammates because he doesn't act like the Big Man on Campus."

Generally speaking, Harbaugh is not one to compare. He doesn't like comparing players, current or past. He doesn't compare games he's played or coached in because he feels like someone or something will be devalued. But he singled out Darboh, who went through the process the previous year of becoming an American citizen, at his position. "I would say he's our top receiver right now," he said. "And as we went through the season last year, I thought that was Jehu Chesson. And then Amara surged during spring ball there, and they're in a very good-hearted competition there to be our best receiver. But, again, as a gentleman, as a person, as a class act, a winner, a champion all the way, Amara Darboh. He went through our season last year and he became an American citizen. It was a great moment of pride for Amara and our team that he achieved American citizenship. And another player on our team, class act the entire way, never an issue, never a problem, respectful to all that he comes in contact with. And not just respectful to people, he's respectful of their time. He's respectful of the game. He's respectful in all forms and fashions."

Harbaugh addressed expectations for the season that had been set so high nearly seven months earlier. Spring practice went well, and for the most part, the Wolverines survived injury-free. "We have big hopes. We've got big dreams. We've got lofty goals," Harbaugh said. "And all those are achievable. And they have to be worked for. You can accomplish anything if the work is realized. And those things have to be earned. So we are in the position right now to work to get the things we want. That's the fact. That's the mentality. That's the attitude."

He relied on some of the concepts he has used before and undoubtedly will use again and he shared his approach. Although reporters wanted him to speak about the race in the East Division, he brought the discussion back to the team and the team alone. "The main focus, the greatest share, the biggest percentage is focusing on getting better each day, better today than yesterday, better tomorrow than today, understanding that improvement will lead to success," said Harbaugh, repeating a favorite slogan before ending with another. "That's the theory, and it's so simple that it just might work."

Harbaugh simply asks his players to improve 1 percent each day, he said. That follows his feeling that everyone needs to be better today than yesterday. And tomorrow is better than today. Harbaugh says that all the time and points out the notion that improvement will lead to success even at small increments, and when it really counts, when it really matters, that gradual improvement will pay off in a big way. "And that's the kind of improvement that really sticks, almost like getting in shape," he said. "If you were getting in shape, if you do it day after day, a little bit, a little bit better, a little bit better each day, you may not see it in a day. You may not see it in a week, you may not even see it in a month, but at some point, you're going to see it, and it's going to stick. That improvement is going to be there for the long run. So trying to paint that picture, if it's 1 percent better each guy, or we got 1 percent better as a team each day, then after 30 days, we'd be 30 percent better. After 60 days we'd be 60 percent better. Now, even if it's can we get .01 percent better each day, then that would be something that would be worthwhile. That would be worth pursuing, aspiring to. Another way to say it is, look at the NASCAR boys. They will try to stay up all night long to get one mile an hour faster. Can we get one mile faster each day? That mentality, simply put, is better today than yesterday, better tomorrow than today."

Those reporters who cover Harbaugh on a regular basis know those theories and they also know all about his feeling that every position on the team is a meritocracy. He spelled that out to the bigger crowd in Chicago who had asked about the freshmen coming in, particularly Rashan Gary, who had so much acclaim coming out of New Jersey. Harbaugh always makes it clear there are no promises when it comes to starting positions. There is not room to take a break or a practice rep off. Those who get on the field are rewarded for their efforts every day in practice. And it doesn't matter if you're a freshman or a fifth-year senior. "That's one of my favorite things, my personal favorite things about our program, is that you'll be known by your effort and your talent," Harbaugh said. "By your effort and your talent, you will be known. So the best players will be the starters, and then the backup roles will be earned. The contributing roles will be earned, the specialty roles will be earned, scout team roles will be earned. It's as simple as that. There are no games, or tricks, or politics, or what class are you in, what year are you, are you on scholarship, are you not on scholarship. It's based upon a meritocracy, the way it should be."

He paused for a moment to inject some humor. "Did I make that word up, too, by the way? Is meritocracy a real word or did I make it up?" he joked. "I thought I made it up."

Harbaugh could not end his remarks without speaking about Peppers, the Big Ten's Freshman of the Year a season before as a redshirt freshman. Peppers had shown he could be a threat on offense and returning kicks and certainly on his defense, where he primarily played.

Harbaugh has seen the very best football players on the professional level and believes they are the greatest athletes in the world. "Jabrill is that kind of athlete," he said. "He's that kind of athlete that has the greatest-in-the-world-type of athleticism. He can play just about anywhere on a football field and be effective. Put him in at corner, put him in at safety, put him in at nickel, put him in at linebacker. Ultimately, probably nickel is his best position. He can be a returner of the punts, returner of the kickoffs, he could be a gunner, he could be a hold-up guy. Offensively, probably right now could probably be our slot receiver and would give De'Veon and all of our running backs a run for their money to be the best running back on the team, could be a wildcat quarterback, could be an outside receiver, can run all the reverses and fly sweeps. So I think you get the picture. He is a tremendous athlete. The other thing about Jabrill is he's highly, highly motivated and very serious about being good. He's seen a lot in his life from an early age. He's felt people try to put him down. He's felt people try to put hate on him from an early age, some about even where he went to high school. He's taken a lot of racial and other type of directive hate toward him. He's never let that get him down or put him down. He's always used that as fuel and motivation. He's a very fiery guy. He is highly motivated, and with the type of athleticism that he has, I truly believe [if] he keeps working and keeps having the same intensity and focus that he's had and the seriousness about being a very good football player and student and all those things, he could explode into a giant of a man."

Michigan hadn't been the buzz in Chicago for several years. Not that the Wolverines were an afterthought, but they certainly hadn't been considered a favorite until Harbaugh arrived.

The previous year in Chicago, he left the stage after addressing the media and was swarmed outside the room and essentially held another news conference. The next day, all of the coaches and their players were seated at individual tables where they would spend a few hours answering questions. Harbaugh was, not unexpectedly, surrounded.

The Harbaugh Hype hadn't died down by the 2016 Big Ten Media Days. In fact, because expectations were so high, that was the main topic of conversation with the players. Butt said that while the four-hour spring practices were eye-opening and offered immediate insight into the man who had taken over the program, he learned something about Harbaugh and his team after the opening-season loss at Utah in 2015. "We played our assess off, and I think if we played them again, we would win," Butt said. "In past years when we lost, one loss would turn into two or three losses. Everyone would be down on themselves. You could kind of feel we were leaning toward that when we got in the locker room [after the game], but Coach Harbaugh looked at all of us and he crushed that right then and there. He told us he was proud of us and proud of the way we played, and we're going to be just fine going down the stretch. We all believed him and we all bought into him at that point. It was such a different feeling coming out of a loss, the next few weeks we played great."

Harbaugh instilled confidence in them, and they began to change their entire approach. Their body language changed, and they also realized it was okay to show some of that confidence and feel good about how far they felt they could go as long as they bought in. "We are a very hard-working team," Butt said. "That's what we want to be known as. We could care less what people pick to be the Big Ten or national champion because at the end of the day none of that really matters. You're either going to be that or you're not. All we can control is what we do, and that's work hard, prepare, and get ready for Week 1. I think we are close to being that. I think we have talent. We have great coaches and we have great leadership in our program. You put those three pieces together and you should have a great season."

Butt was the first to say in the spring that Michigan would be a national contender in Harbaugh's second season. Even in the deep East Division with Ohio State and Michigan State, who had won the division a year earlier, and up-and-coming Penn State, he said the Wolverines were not worried at all.

Interestingly, he referenced the offseason commotion Harbaugh had created on the college football scene. While Harbaugh deftly side-stepped the topic during his interviews, Butt made it clear that the Wolverines knew the attention they had received probably irked their rivals and the rest of college football. "I don't think we're chasing anybody," Butt said. "I don't think we fear anybody, or we worry about anybody or we're trying to play catch up. I think we realize we probably do have a target on our back just from how much attention this program gets for different things we've been doing. I think there is going to be a target on our back. Even before that, even in my first two years, teams would come into Michigan Stadium, and it would make their season to beat us. That's what we expect."

The Wolverines certainly were feeling good about their defense with so many veterans coming back, and guys like Taco Charlton and Chris Wormley saying Michigan was going to have the best defensive line in the country. But breaking in a new quarterback is not exactly easy, and at that point, less than two weeks before the start of camp, a starter had not yet been determined, though Wilton Speight was ahead after the spring game.

There was a difference, though, and it was the fact there was stability in the offensive staff. The trio of Harbaugh, offensive coordinator Tim Drevno, and pass-game coordinator Jedd Fisch all called the plays, and each of those coaches returned. For an offense that had played for three coordinators in three years, this was a welcome dose of familiarity. Mostly, they had started to understand Harbaugh. "When he first came in here, it was a shock to us, and he got us out of our comfort zone a little bit," Butt said. "But going into Year Two, we understand a little bit about how he works."

No one *really* knows how Harbaugh works, but the players had picked up his edge. He doesn't care what other people say about what he's doing or what his team is doing, and Butt said that's how the players were feeling. They understood how high expectations had become, partly because they helped fan those flames, and they were just fine with it. Harbaugh had told them every week would be a championship week, and that's how they became programmed. Certain games would be bigger, of course, like the rivalry games against Michigan State and Ohio State, but the reality was, Harbaugh wanted Rutgers week to feel the same as either of those two weeks.

Buoyed by the confidence with which Harbaugh had equipped the players, Butt said they knew that the hard work coming up in the brutal weeks of preseason camp—a continuation of their work in winter conditioning, spring practice, and voluntary summer workouts—would ultimately pay off in the end. "There's definitely hype within the team, but it's not from what other people are saying," he said. "We're kind of building our own hype because of the work

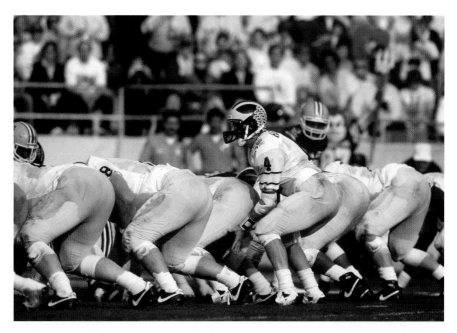

Jim Harbaugh's ties to Michigan include quarterbacking the Wolverines to an 11–2 record in 1986 and a Rose Bowl berth. (USA TODAY Sports Images)

Bo Schembechler, who yells at Jim Harbaugh during the Rose Bowl, is often cited by Harbaugh as a valuable, but tough, mentor. (AP Images)

*(From left to right) brother John Harbaugh, father Jack Harbaugh, grandfather Joe Cipiti, mother Jackie Harbaugh, and Jim Harbaugh pose before Super Bowl XLVII, which was known as the "Harbowl" because Jim and John's teams faced off. (*USA TODAY *Sports Images)*

A billboard outside of The Big House welcomes Jim Harbaugh home in late December of 2014. (AP Images)

During the December 30, 2014, press conference announcing the hiring of Jim Harbaugh as head coach, (from left to right) former Michigan head coach Lloyd Carr, interim athletic director Jim Hackett, Harbaugh, and former Michigan head coach Gary Moeller pose for a group photo. (USA TODAY Sports Images)

In its first year under Jim Harbaugh, Michigan celebrates its 41–7 thrashing of Florida in the Citrus Bowl. (AP Images)

Just over a month after winning the Citrus Bowl, Michigan hosted a "Signing of the Stars" extravaganza during Signing Day, which included Derek Jeter (far left, with microphone) and Tom Brady (front row, middle), among other celebrities and Michigan fans. (AP Images)

In Bradenton, Florida, the Michigan coaches work with Cheyenn Robertson during one of the satellite camps, which has drawn the ire of coaches at rival programs. (AP Images)

In honor of Michigan becoming the first football program to wear his Jumpman logo, Michael Jordan served as a captain before the Hawaii game. (AP Images)

Don Brown became the defensive coordinator for the 2016 season, and his intensity is matched only by Jim Harbaugh. (AP Images)

Michigan had a spirited quarterback competition in 2016, in which Wilton Speight (right) beat out John O'Korn (left). (AP Images)

An All-American and senior defensive leader in 2016, cornerback Jourdan Lewis readies to play Penn State, which Michigan defeated 49–10. (AP Images)

Senior Jake Butt, who had 546 receiving yards during the 2016 season, takes off after one of his four catches against Penn State. (AP Images)

we've been putting in this offseason. Going into camp we're starting to feel a little bit more confident about what we've got going on this team. Everybody is excited to get into camp and start working and playing some real football again. Going into my senior year, I've been with most of the guys in my class three, four years. This is the reason we all came together as a class. *If* we put in the work this year, we work hard, we prepare the way I know we're capable of, we can have a real special season. You can't win the Big Ten championship without winning the game right in front of you. You can't get to the college football playoff without winning Game 1. We're going to have a target on our back this fall and we know that. Everyone that comes into our stadium is going to be playing their best against us and trying to knock us off. We saw that last year. We fought in some really close games. Some of them we lost, some of them we won. The goal this year is to win them all."

5

Submergence

BEFORE HIS FIRST SEASON AT MICHIGAN, JIM Harbaugh decided to take his team into what he called "the submarine" for preseason camp. It made sense for team building and toughening the players, but by no means was it media friendly. After all, there was little that came out of the football building for three weeks, which is exactly how Harbaugh wanted it. Just ahead of the 2016 season, he said he had not yet decided if the team would go submarine again unless he said, someone sticks bamboo shoots under his fingernails. "Then maybe I'll have to," Harbaugh said, laughing.

Fans and media long for morsels of information during preseason camp, but that is never his concern. Harbaugh liked the results from the previous season's submarine for a number of reasons. "That gives our team the right and the ability to improve, make mistakes, and correct and learn from those mistakes within a team concept," Harbaugh said. "I think a player and a team have the right to do that. When you're at the beginning, I think it's very good and beneficial to work together as a team, with the team only. It was fun. You have to understand: that's the [most fun] time of the year. That's when your team is forged."

It was forged without distraction. And that first camp was particularly important for Harbaugh and his staff. Yes, they had gone through a spring practice with the team, but this was fall camp, less than a month before the season, and all the freshmen were in. This is when so much happens, and so much focus is needed. "When you're around each other, and there's not anyone else in the facility, you can concentrate on what you need to learn and how you need to do it," Michigan offensive coordinator Tim Drevno said in 2015.

"You can build a relationship with your coaches and really get to know your teammates, get that trust. It's a real fun time."

The team was fully submerged. They would find out late the night before via text what the next day's schedule would be. But there was little for them outside of football and more football. "We had no idea what was going on in the outside world," offensive lineman Kyle Kalis said after that first camp. "It's been an experience that I will tell my kids about. It's definitely been a camp we have never had before. I think that is going to pay off in dividends this year. We have come together as a team really well. We are super tight."

Before Harbaugh's arrival, the Michigan players stayed at the Sheraton hotel and went to practices. Under Harbaugh they lived in dorms without air conditioning. So much for the country club. "Before we were living good," Kalis said. "We had nice puffy beds, nice warm food in the morning, getting some nice coffee if you wanted it."

Harbaugh had them living in close quarters. "Got really tight with the boys," Kalis said. "Overall, it was a really good thing for us. You wake up in the morning, you do football. It's football, eat, football, eat, workout, eat, football, eat, practice, eat, sleep. It's nonstop."

When Media Day came around in early August, players were giddily preparing for the season and still talking up their goals and expectations just as they had been at the end of spring practice. As preseason camp was about to begin, Harbaugh, being less committal regarding his team going into submarine mode, spoke as he typically does this time of season. "It's one of two special times to me in the entire calendar," Harbaugh said to the roomful of media. "I've said it before: a lot of people look at January 1st being the start of the new year. People look—those who espouse Christianity, Catholicism—look at Christmas as the start of the liturgical year, but us in football, first day of preseason camp is the new year. It's like being reborn into football, coming out of the womb into the bright light, into the chaos, into everybody look at you. It's where a team is forged, under the sun in the August heat. Sun shaping the body, carving the mind. Very excited."

Media Day is always a fun day for the players. They get their photos taken and they're all available for interviews. Just a few days earlier, Michigan fans had lined up, some for hours and hours, to get a chance to be the first to purchase the new Nike gear. And Media Day was the first time the players donned their new Nike Jordan Jumpman uniforms publicly. They were big fans of the jerseys with the Jumpman logo on the left chest and excitedly spoke of meeting Michael Jordan for the first game of the season when he would be honorary captain. "I'm happy about it," running back De'Veon Smith said. "I get to meet Michael Jordan the first game. It's on my bucket list. It's kind of a humbling experience to meet such a great athlete and to be wearing that logo and be the first team, really. But the only thing is, we can't get lost in the logo. We've got to focus on exactly what our goals are and what we need to do." Jabrill Peppers echoed the same message. "I appreciate the gear and all that, but we've still got to win games in it," Peppers said.

Harbaugh reiterated the thrill of the night of the Nike launch. He praised the product and said the Jordan Brand had "knocked our socks off." "I was dazzled," Harbaugh said, reliving that midnight launch. "It felt like a victory celebration. It felt like a championship celebration. It also motivated me personally and other guys that I've talked to on the team and on the staff. You know, 'Let's win a championship and do one of these, shut down State Street,' and that's what it's all about."

Peppers, understandably, was a hot topic during Media Day. If Michigan was going to pursue a championship, he would be a large part of that. He was a three-way threat the previous season, and cornerback Jourdan Lewis, who also returned kicks, had decided he wanted in on some offense. He had brought up that possibility in Chicago during Big Ten Media Days, and Harbaugh made it clear Lewis could join Peppers as the Wolverines' three-way threats.

"I love having the ball in my hands," Lewis said. "I love being out there trying to make plays. I'm a little Antonio Brown. I can run some routes. I think I'm a pretty good route runner."

Peppers liked the idea and praised Lewis' hands. "I don't know why they haven't been letting Jourdan play both ways," Peppers said. "Jourdan is one of the craziest athletes I've ever seen. We definitely favor each other a lot. We just have different body types and playing styles. Jourdan can be just as efficient on offense as he is on defense. I've covered him; he's covered me. We speak from experience when we say that. People can have trouble with Jourdan on offense, just as they do on defense. I hope they give him a shot. It would be nice to have a fellow defensive man over there...But at the end of the day, we may not need him over there, or they may need him over there. Always wrenches we can throw in there, so we like to keep the opposition guessing."

The known three-way player, though, was Peppers. He had shifted in the spring to a new defensive role under new coordinator Don Brown and was initially listed as a linebacker/defensive back on the first roster of the season. But, really, there was no way to categorize him. Even Peppers could not be specific when it came to his position. "I just say 'athlete,'" Peppers said. "I don't really get into specifics."

It is difficult to confine Peppers in one role, but that's always been his norm. "I've been doing that since Pop Warner," Peppers said. "I don't know why people make a big deal out of that. I'm just playing football. I guess it's because it's at this level. It's not as hard as you guys make it seem to be, just get my plays in and try to execute. I guess [the coaches] see the capability. I just look at it as I've been doing this since Pop Warner and high school, and they trust me to do it now. I just thought it would behoove me to play the best that I can play for my team and myself. That's how I look at it. I don't look at it like, 'He can do this, he can do that.' I'm just playing football. Everything is football for me."

Ideally, Harbaugh said he wanted to keep Peppers in the range of 90-95 plays a game with 100 being the very top he would go. Harbaugh has said on multiple occasions that Peppers picked up on plays almost instantly. They show him what they want him to run, and he can immediately follow through. It all seemed so easy and uncomplicated for Peppers, and Harbaugh said he never had to keep it simple for Peppers because of his sixth sense for football. "I've seen very few athletes with the ability to just show it to him on a white board, maybe show him a clip what you want him to do, and then for him to go right out to the practice field and do it better than anyone else on the team or better than you thought he could do it. He's one of those rare guys. Andrew Luck [who Harbaugh coached at Stanford] was that kind of athlete and had that kind of mind. You just had to tell him, and he could do it. You told him sometimes midway through practice with Andrew, and he would do it right and he would do it perfect. We would tell Jabrill sometimes midway through practice, 'We didn't cover this in the meeting, but here's what we want you to do, here's what we're calling the play. Run over after five plays on defense, and we're going to line you up at tailback,' and he lines up without a walk-through rep or without a study in a meeting and can execute it better than you thought. Really, those two guys are the only two I can think of that are like that, that have that kind of sharpness of mind and athletic ability. It takes real supreme athletic ability to have someone to tell you to do something, and you to just do it. That's at a different level. That's off the charts."

Peppers' teammates often couldn't find the words to describe the kind of player he is. "He's very adaptive," Lewis said. "He's like a chameleon out there. He understands what he needs to do and where he needs to be every single time. He barely has missed assignments. That's wild [considering] all the positions he plays. He can do everything. He's one of those special players you don't find too often."

Peppers had aspired to be like former Wolverine Charles Woodson, who in 1997 became the first primarily defensive player to win the Heisman Trophy. Woodson kept tabs on Peppers and frequently texted him, especially if he saw something in a game he thought he could help correct or improve. "He just keeps me grounded," Peppers said. "He's one of the best to do it, so he gives me advice, things that just keep me up. I texted him a lot during spring ball when I was going through the transition of playing so many different positions, and he was there to help me out."

A conversation with Peppers, even before the season started, couldn't avoid the elephant in the room—would this be his final season at Michigan? As a redshirt junior, he would be able to declare for the NFL after the season. He wanted no part of that discussion. "I'm a college athlete right now," he said. "That's what my main focus is—with the University of Michigan. I'm not thinking about anything I can't control. I learned that lesson my freshman year when I got hurt trying to look too far into the future. I'm just focused on right now, right now. That's just going out and having the best season I can possibly have."

Media Days lend themselves to goofiness, as well, and right tackle Erik Magnuson had a major announcement to make. "They're moving the right tackle to quarterback starting the 2016 season," he said. "Erik Magnuson will be starting at quarterback for the University of Michigan." It would be a joke made by his teammates that would continue to be made several weeks into the season.

Not a joking matter, however, was the status of the offensive line. The Wolverines were returning four starting offensive linemen, including Mason Cole, who had started all 25 games of his career at left tackle, and had moved to center. That made room for a new face at left tackle, sophomore Grant Newsome, who had made one career start.

Magnuson, a fifth-year senior, had made 24 starts and was All-Big Ten third team the previous season; Kyle Kalis, a fifth-year senior right guard, had made 29 starts and also was third-team All-Big Ten; and left guard Ben Braden, a senior, had made 25 starts and was All-Big Ten honorable mention. Kalis didn't mince words when assessing how good the line will be with that core group. "It's going to be damn good," Kalis said. "This is going to be one of the best lines we've had at Michigan for a while now. I'm not just saying that, just to say it. The way we've come together this offseason especially with player-led practices, we're on. Everything we're seeing, we're just on."

He clicked his fingers for emphasis when saying the offensive line is "on" and then noted how much Michigan's early home schedule can add to their confidence. "You're going to see it the first five games at home," Kalis said. "The first test is to do everything we can to be over and beyond. We're going to be damn good, yeah."

Measuring an offensive line with statistics can be difficult. The linemen often point at rushing totals, but perhaps the most telling stat the last three seasons had been sacks allowed. In 2013 Michigan had four different line combinations through the season, and Kalis and Magnuson earned some starts. The group was ranked 105th nationally in sacks allowed, giving up 36.

The line improved in 2014, allowing 25 sacks to rank 76th, and in 2016, Drevno's first season coaching the line, the group saw generous improvement and was tied for 27th in sacks allowed, giving up 18.

Center Graham Glasgow, drafted to the NFL by the Detroit Lions, was an enormous loss from the 2015 offensive line, but Kalis said there was a sense that even with the new addition of Newsome that the line was finally at a point that it could be a strength of the team. That was something no one could have said the previous few seasons, but with Drevno returning, lending a layer of coaching consistency, the players felt confident. Certainly, they were older and experienced and with that comes some swagger, but having quality coaching gave them a boost. "Everything this past couple of years, everything is coming together," Kalis said. "Everything is falling into place. It's like a storybook ending. It would be amazing to end our last season here the way we thought coming in it was going to be. That's what's happening. It's awesome."

Another measure of a line's production involves the run game. Michigan wasn't the most consistent in 2015, averaging 158.2 yards, but a strong performance in the bowl victory against Florida gave the returning starters a place to start. The Wolverines had 225 rushing yards and two rushing touchdowns in the bowl, and Smith gained 109 yards.

Smith, the hard-nosed runner, was pleased with what he would be running behind in the fall. "I'm happy about it," Smith said. "You get, basically, the entire offensive line back. We did big things last year, and that was our first time in the offense. The second year is going to be a lot easier for them. They're going to be taking steps, making their blocks faster, and the holes are going to be even bigger. I have high expectations for our offensive line."

And so did the offensive line. As a group, they were determined to obviously protect the quarterback, whoever it would be, but also to make larger holes for the running backs. "We're going to be better in the run game. We all want to be better in the run game," Magnuson said. "That's a big emphasis Coach Drevno's putting on there. We want to be able to dominate a game from start to finish, so I think we're going to be really good. We have the players, we have the coach, we've gotta make it happen. We've played together, and that's huge. We all have a lot of game experience, and experience is the biggest thing in sports."

The only newbie was Newsome, who was young and entering his sophomore season but also massive at 6'7", 318 pounds. "With Grant I think it's just a maturity thing," Kalis said. "Being a young guy and if you don't already come in with the mental edge, it's one of those things you've got to learn to be able to flip the switch when you're called upon. He'll find that eventually. It's a matter of time.

Hopefully it will be faster."

Speaking of young guys, while Peppers was the talk of Media Day, not far behind was Rashan Gary. The nation's top recruit in the nation came out of Paramus (New Jersey) Catholic, the same school that produced Peppers. He had already started to feel legendary around the Michigan campus, even though he hadn't taken a snap. Lewis had described the 6'5", 287-pound Gary as being light on his feet for a big guy, who could, he said, dance his way through the ladder drill. Tight end Jake Butt had marveled that Gary had benched 26 reps of 225 pounds shortly before Media Day. And many of his older defensive line teammates, like Maurice Hurst, expressed gratitude that Gary has been attentive and eager to learn from his older linemates instead of acting like the Big Freshman On Campus.

Defensive line coach Greg Mattison had absolutely no hesitation saying Gary would be a factor in the fall, sooner rather than later, despite the amount of veteran talent returning. "I believe what I saw of him in high school, what I've seen of him just training, what I've heard from our veterans who are with him, he definitely has the ability, the maturity, and that's the key," Mattison said. "There's a lot of freshmen over the years who could play early, but they're just not ready maturity-wise. He seems to be ready that way."

Michigan linebackers coach Chris Partridge coached Gary at Paramus Catholic before joining Harbaugh's staff in 2015. Partridge agreed with Mattison's assessment of Gary's maturity and said he had made a quick adjustment to college. "Me and Rashan are always going to have a different relationship than anyone else here because I've known him for a long time. I know his family and am really close to him," Partridge said. "He'll come to me with certain things and questions, but he's transitioned. He's ready to rock. He had a great summer and feels really good."

Mattison said Gary's ability to blend with his teammates so quickly has been an enormous plus. "I've been very impressed with how humble he's been and how much he has moved in with the other guys and said, 'Okay, what do you want me to do? I'm going to do it that way,'" Mattison said. "He has stopped up [in the office] and asked me questions at times on the playbook, so he's obviously been with [Chris] Wormley and those guys going through the defenses. A couple things he wasn't sure of, he asked me, got it, 'Okay, Coach,' gone. Of all the freshmen over my years I've seen, he seems very mature and very committed to being a Michigan Man."

All this talk of Peppers and offensive linemen improvements and Gary, but what about the quarterback situation? Harbaugh wasn't revealing much. It appeared to be a two-man race between Wilton Speight and John O'Korn, the transfer from Houston who had impressed the coaches the previous season as he led the scout-team offense. Speight had the edge coming out of the spring, but there was still plenty of talk out there about O'Korn.

After all, Jake Rudock was a transfer and he started, so there seemed to be an assumption that O'Korn, who sat out the previous season per transfer rules, would follow a similar path.

Although he said he would prefer to defer giving his opinion on the quarterback race until the start of the season, Harbaugh did shed a tiny bit of light, albeit vague, on the two. "They're our two front-runners coming out of spring practice competing for the job," Harbaugh said. "[The] thing I like about both of them is how important it is to both those young men as players in the competitive situation that they're in, and they're embracing it."

And on the eve of the first day of camp, Harbaugh said he didn't care much for outside expectations. Would he address the team about them? Probably not. Did he think that might be an issue for the players, and they'd get full of themselves? Again, probably not. "Those outside expectations and perceptions, they do rise and fall with the day," Harbaugh said. "Sometimes by the hour. So as I said before, our expectations are going to be very high. As a coach my expectations are very high for practice, the meetings, installations, the drills, and practice, scrimmaging, and competition."

That would be the start of the real new year for Harbaugh, the day he eagerly awaits each season. The players would begin to work toward starting roles, and his plan included never allowing them to settle or stop working. Dan Dierdorf—a former All-American offensive tackle at Michigan under Bo Schembechler, a two-time Hall of Famer (college and NFL), and radio analyst for the Wolverines' games—said he witnessed something very familiar watching Harbaugh coach practices.

Dierdorf often feels transported back in time while watching Harbaugh coach, knowing that so much of what he is doing now was learned from Schembechler and reinvented with his own twist. Even calling competition and earning playing time a "meritocracy," that was derived from playing for Schembechler. "Bo made it very clear to every one of us you have to earn your spot on this team every day," Dierdorf said. "Bo would make everybody so aware of the fact that nothing was more important than the team. If you in any way did anything, whether that was off the field, the way you did the summer job he got you, the way you went to class, he made it known, if you didn't uphold your end of the bargain, you were out. You weren't going to play. Anybody who played for Bo Schembechler, no one ever used the world 'entitled.' There was never favorites. He made it known the only favorite to him was the team. We bought into that.

"Let me tell you, Bo's guys were the ones who practiced the hardest and played the best. Jim Harbaugh is doing the same thing. Nobody is playing because of how well they played last year. Nobody is playing in November because they had a great September. Uh uh. That's not how he works. He's his own man and has his own strategies, but I'm telling you, there's a lot of Bo in Jim Harbaugh in the team building. I can see a whole lot of it."

And so the team building for Harbaugh's second team at Michigan would continue to build during the wear-you-down heat and humidity of August and preseason camp.

6

Dr. Blitz's First Preseason

A S PRESEASON CAMP WORE ON, IT BECAME VERY CLEAR that the 2016 season was not taking on the same submarine quality of the previous year. Jim Harbaugh himself surfaced early on and was available only briefly, but the players had opportunities to mingle with media and share thoughts on where things stood week to week.

There the Wolverines were, hitting the practice field ahead of Harbaugh's second season as coach, and still *the* question popped up again. For whatever reason, even though there had been no indications Harbaugh had been anything but happy to be in Ann Arbor, questions about his future always managed to find their way into interviews with national media. There is no question that many observers outside the program think Harbaugh ultimately will have a short stay in Ann Arbor coaching the Wolverines because he will have the itch to return to the NFL. There's all that unfinished business, especially after losing the Super Bowl to his brother. For whatever reason, it is impossible for most outside of the Michigan fold to believe this job can satisfy his coaching aspirations. During an appearance on Sirius XM College Sports that aired during camp, he was asked if he "legitimately" sees himself "coaching Michigan forever." The hosts asked if Michigan is the "ultimate job for you 20-25 years from now."

"Do you think that way?" he was asked.

Harbaugh didn't hesitate. "Yeah, I think that way," Harbaugh said, sounding upbeat. "And I think, God willing and the creek don't rise, that will happen. I love coaching, I love football, I *love* the University of Michigan, and you hope to go as long as you can where you're still doing it by example, not just through anecdote, and you're still able to do that as long as the good Lord will allow you to do it."

Often, people from the outside have wondered if he's too intense, whether that can last, and if assistant coaches can handle the grind of working for him. Harbaugh told the radio show he had not detected that at Michigan or any other coaching stop. "I can't really think of a time where it's been too much," he said. "I've always thought more is more anyway. Maybe I'm the wrong guy to talk to about that. When people make that assertion, it's like, 'What is it? What are you talking about? And we can go through that one by one.'"

With the Wolverines at the midway point of preseason camp and the season opener against Hawaii nearing, Harbaugh said they were working hard and had continued to prepare in every phase. Had he been walking while conducting the interview, people would have said he had a bounce in his step. While outsiders had been hyping his program, he was simply hyped for the season. "You create it, you have at it, and you do it," he said. "I think all the listeners can identify to it. Where can you go to get that [kind of competition]? I hate to compare humans to animals, but that's how I always felt—like the thoroughbreds at the Kentucky Derby. When they come out, they hear the bugler's call, they start getting into a lather, the jockeys say the horse's heart starts pounding, the eyes bulge. That's how I feel. It's time to race. It's time to compete. Gosh, where can you find that? You can find it in football, that I know. It's fun to see that look in the youngsters who are out there competing for something. To be a part of that is great. Coaching's the next best thing that I've found. Playing's the best because you're out there doing it, but coaching is the best."

In the midst of its preseason camp tour of all the conference schools, The Big Ten Network drove its specially designed bus to Ann Arbor and took in a practice. Harbaugh keeps practices limited to the outside world, so the BTN's day to observe and share video clips was that rare cookie crumb everyone tried to grab to get satiated for that final push toward the start of the season.

Gerry DiNardo, a BTN analyst, admittedly was not one of those who bought into the preseason love and hype Michigan had been receiving since early in the year. He certainly wasn't buying into projections of the Wolverines being in the four-team national playoff. But when he and his fellow BTN analysts Dave Revsine and Howard Griffith left practice, he had a vastly different opinion. "This is not what I expected," DiNardo said shortly afterward. "I went into the tour saying Michigan is overrated. I'm backing off that. I think they're rated accurately. I thought because of all the offseason publicity people bought into that because of all that attention. They're absolutely better than I thought."

They had already visited Ohio State, and considering the fact they all believed Michigan State would be down, DiNardo predicted the East Division would come down to Michigan and Ohio State in the final regular-season game. "I've seen Ohio State, and [players] one through 85 may be more talented [than Michigan], but you can't play all 85...They can be as good as anybody. Do they have as much talent as Ohio State? Again, I don't think there's that much difference. I don't think Ohio State beats them because they have more talent. I don't think Michigan wins because of more talent. We're back to whoever plays better in that game. [The Wolverines] have closed the gap."

He and Griffith tend to start with the offensive and defensive lines when they're making evaluations. "If you look at Michigan's offensive and defensive lines, you come to the conclusion they can block anybody they play and stop anybody they play," DiNardo said. "They're deeper in the offensive line than they've been, and we've been following some of these young guys for several years."

Defensively, DiNardo agreed with most assessments that Michigan's line and secondary would be exceptionally strong, but that the linebackers lacked depth and experience. He made a point to single out freshman Rashan Gary, the highly lauded defensive line recruit. "He's the real deal. He's going to play," DiNardo said. "We saw Peppers when he was a freshman, and the difference between him and Peppers—Peppers was so much more mature. Gary is a very good kid, a great body, impressive in drills. During the team period, they rushed the passer, the quarterback would throw, and he will stand there and then start running. He'll grow every day. [Defensive line coach Greg] Mattison will show him the tape and tell him, 'Rashan, when the quarterback throws, you have to run downfield.' He'll see the older guys never stop running. That first year, you would have thought Peppers was a senior, he got it."

Players like Gary and Peppers, not to mention the quarterback battle, caught DiNardo's attention, but so too did Don Brown, as the new defensive coordinator. He wondered how Brown would call defenses early in the season against a not-so-threatening non-conference schedule of teams. Would he hold back? "It will be interesting how the defense evolves," DiNardo said. "How high risk it's going to be will be interesting. I think he'll find his niche, but his niche here doesn't have to be the same exact niche he had at BC."

In his overall assessment, he said he wasn't surprised that in Harbaugh's second season the Wolverines could be legitimate contenders. "Brady [Hoke] was recruiting good players," DiNardo said. "At Rutgers Kyle Flood left Chris Ash a decent roster. It does have something to do with who you're following as a coach. Brady did a good job. It's not really the second year of personnel development. It's the second year of the new culture."

Although Harbaugh inherited some pretty good talent when he took the Michigan job, he and his staff also went out and recruited hard and landed top-notch personnel. Gary was the one grabbing the headlines, but early in camp, Harbaugh singled out Detroit-product Michael Onwenu, a massive human being he called one of his "favorites." Onwenu could play offensive or defensive line, but his flexibility in terms of where he could be used did not outweigh his—well—weight. He arrived in Ann Arbor at 6'3" and about 380 pounds, and his teammates marveled at his stature. "He's a mountain of a man. He's a big guy," Ryan Glasgow, a 299-pound senior nose tackle said, smiling. "I think that's the heaviest on the team by about 50 pounds. That's a pretty wide margin on a college football team."

Heading into the season, though, it just wasn't about the players. Although Brown impressed plenty during spring practice as Michigan's new defensive coordinator and had seemingly passed all the tests—including having the coolest mustache as determined by the players—he remained the most talked-about new hire. The Michigan players marveled at Brown's high-intensity, high energy approach to practices. How could a 61-year-old man, considered old to teenagers and young 20-somethings, be this electrified and emotionally charged. "Sixty-one going on 21 is the running joke," Glasgow said. "He hops in drills. He's way more hands-on than I would expect. It's really refreshing to see someone that hands-on."

Safety Dymonte Thomas said the players appreciated how involved Brown—also affectionately known to them as Dr. Blitz—was in practices and how much time he spent teaching them. The players say D.J. Durkin, his predecessor, was equally as enthusiastic but more of a yeller, and Brown was calmer. "He's here, he's there, he's always, boom! boom! 'What are we doing? Let's go! All right, bring it in,'" Thomas said. "He's always excited, he's always moving. He looks like he's 21 out there on the field, but after we get back in a meeting, he's calmed down, he's more relaxed, and he's more chill. He's really out there on the field with us yelling, screaming, having fun, jumping around with us."

The older you get in a young person's profession, however, the more tired you grow when people talk about your age. Brown, frankly, had grown tired of it long before he took the job at Michigan. Sure, everyone knows what year he was born and how long he's been coaching, but age means nothing to him. "I've heard that age thing; it makes me nauseous," Brown said. "Bring anybody in here,

I'll be glad to match [them and] put my energy level with anybody else's. I take pride in going out on the field. I think I'll be one of those guys, when I can't do that, I'll probably go."

Brown in many ways resembles the all-out, aggressive, unrelenting defense he runs. He's nicknamed Dr. Blitz for a reason after all. And as he likes to say, he wants his players to solve their on-field problems with aggression. "We'll blitz no matter where we are on the field and what down it is, which is really awesome because when you blitz like that you get an opportunity to get your hands on the ball," Thomas said. "Coach Brown is not scared to pressure a quarterback and create pressure throughout the game, so that quarterback is going to get tired and he'll continue to throw the ball up."

Brown easily shows his feelings and his irritations. When DiNardo's comments got back to him about running a high-risk, high-reward defense, he animatedly disagreed. "Whoa, whoa, whoa, that's a bunch of baloney," Brown said, angrily. "High risk? No. We just don't throw this stuff against the wall. Come on, we're not doing that. We look at the formations, we look at the personnel groups. We lean to be on the aggressive side. Whether you're running or passing the ball, we're going to have the ability when we dictate [what's to] come. That's what it's all about. I can assure you that every one of the calls that we've made, we've done a kind of a thorough study. We'll at least have run it 100 times, okay? So we're not throwing things against the wall. It's not that kind of scenario."

Brown pointed out that because they're playing man coverage some misconstrue the high-risk aspect. "We deny free access. We're not going to play eight to 10 yards off and let you play that game all the time. Now, you'll see us play off, but we determine when we do that. We're going to be able to do it all, but I can assure you, I'm not looking at, 'Oh, okay, they're going to run the zone read, and we're going to just throw this one against the wall and see if it works. Too old for that."

As preseason camp continued, Michigan athletic director Warde Manuel, a former Michigan football player whose career ended because of a neck injury and who earned multiple degrees including a PhD, hosted a roundtable discussion, an ask-anything type of session, with reporters. Manuel spoke about a new football weight room, season-ticket waiting lists, and night games. But it is always impossible, it seems, to avoid the topic of his head football coach, who seemingly is the figurehead and most powerful individual in the Michigan athletic department.

Manuel neither agreed with nor argued that point. "Jim Harbaugh is a great colleague in this department," Manuel said. "You guys can determine who's more powerful and all-seeing and all-knowing. That's not for me. Jim is a great colleague, he's a great head coach of our football program. He's a powerful figure in the university and he's a powerful figure in intercollegiate athletics and in football because he's the head coach at Michigan. He's had a tremendous career, he is very bright. So you guys can put however you want to frame it, but I know he's a great colleague to work with."

Asked if he feels he has to keep Harbaugh on a proverbial leash, considering his Twitter activity and some of his bold moves that frequently get under the skin of rivals, Manuel said he treats all of his coaches the same. They are entitled to run their programs as they see fit—within reason, of course—but Manuel does not try to control. He manages, and that goes for how he works with Harbaugh. "I don't have him on a leash, first of all," Manuel said. "I don't have leashes. That's not the way I manage people. If there are things that I need to talk to Jim about, I talk to Jim about it. If there are things I need to talk to other coaches, I talk to them about it, but I don't have leashes and I don't look at it as anything I need to control. I look at it as me helping this department manage effectively and put out there effectively what we're trying to do. I don't give anybody limits. We talk about things as they come up. I think the things that Jim has done have come up in the media. You guys react to it in different ways, our fans react to it in different ways, but Jim has been tremendous to deal with, very smart, very knowledgeable. So when issues come up that we need to talk about it, we talk about it. When something I say or policy or something I implement comes up and he wants to talk to me about it, we talk about it, just like any other coach. He's been tremendous to deal with. I let people be themselves. Jim has his own limits that he sets on what he does and he understands the rules. He understands the Michigan culture. I have to make sure all my coaches are educated on the rules. I have to make sure all my coaches have a sense of the culture. I need to make sure that we have those discussions as a group, individually when necessary. I want Jim Harbaugh to be Jim Harbaugh."

Harbaugh has worked tirelessly since taking the job at his alma mater. He has challenged the NCAA at times by taking his team to Florida for spring break and because of his exhaustive summer satellite camp tours and he has created plenty of controversy and debate. He clearly does not mind mixing it up and he enjoys thinking out of the box and implementing fresh takes. Many national writers have described Harbaugh as a master of the subtweet, taking aim at a subject and getting in a dig with skilled subtlety without ever naming names. He has been adept at utilizing social media to announce birthdays and visits with celebrities but also has used Twitter to poke at national media members and coaching colleagues, almost always generating headlines because of that activity.

Manuel has no interest in stifling or muzzling Harbaugh. "It's a lot of attention on him, but he garnered a lot of attention when he was head coach at San Francisco," Manuel said. "He garnered, I don't know if it's as much, attention when he was at Stanford. I don't mind it. It doesn't bother me. It is what it is. When I look at the coverage and what he's doing and what's out there about him and the program, it has a great deal of positive to it from my perspective. I don't sit down with him and say, 'Jim, I need you to do more' and I don't tell him to do less. He's doing what he's comfortable doing, and there's nothing at this point that would cause me any concern about the amount of coverage or the things that are being covered. Call it what it is. He's doing some things, but most of the coverage is coverage by the media. It's not Jim saying, every day putting out a story or saying, 'Hey, I want you to shoot a video of me every day.'"

Harbaugh draws attention on a nearly daily basis, and some of that stems from the large contract he signed with Michigan. During the month of preseason camp, the addendum to Harbaugh's contract was released. It gave him an additional $2 million annually to his $5 million annual base. But that included a twist that Hackett, who brought this contract device from the corporate world, listed it in the form of a life insurance policy, and the University of Michigan pays a premium of $2 million a year to the insurer for the life of the contract through December 2021.

According to the addendum, Harbaugh was to get two payments of $2 million on separate dates in 2016, which meant he made $9 million for the year. This insurance policy addendum was an important component to the contract for Hackett, and he was delighted the university worked with him on it. This way Harbaugh owns the insurance policy, and if he is coaching the Wolverines on December 6 each year through 2021, the university makes the $2 million annual premium payment to the insurance company. As the policy owner, Harbaugh can make withdrawals or loans from it. Michigan will get its money back without interest upon his death.

It became clear almost immediately after Harbaugh was hired— before he had ever drawn an X and O on a white board—that he was going to give Michigan plenty for the money they were spending. On the sideline of a Baltimore Ravens game in 2015, he wore a black puffy jacket with a block M, and the M Den was flooded with calls the next day requesting to purchase it.

With or without the 10-win season in 2015 that inspired the Michigan fanbase after it had experienced the low from the previous season, Harbaugh moved the needle. For instance, in a 30-day snapshot of mainstream media mentions during the offseason shortly after he was hired, Harbaugh's name was referenced three times more often than Ohio State coach Urban Meyer or Alabama coach Nick Saban.

That's what Eric Wright, president and executive director of Ann Arbor-based Joyce Julius, a sports sponsorship research firm that evaluates corporate sponsorship, found. Harbaugh even had an edge over New England Patriots coach Bill Belichick, who had just won a Super Bowl. Wright's analysis did not provide the reasons why Harbaugh moved the needle, but it definitely offered evidence he does. "Michigan has always been a lightning rod for coverage," Wright said. "But he's taking it to a new level."

More than a year later, national data continued to show that Harbaugh, with all of the headlines he had generated, was more popular than Saban among millennial males (18-34), according to The Q Scores Company, which measures the awareness and appeal of personalities.

Reported in August 2016 by the Associated Press, the data indicated that nearly three-fourths of male sports fans between the ages of 18 and 34 are aware of Jim Harbaugh. His "Q score" was 25 among that group, which means that one in four men in that age group indicated Harbaugh was a favorite of theirs. Saban's Q rating was 21 among those millennial men. "Harbaugh is making a significantly stronger impact than Saban among younger males, and that seems to be his objective," Henry Schafer, executive vice president of The Q Scores, told the Associated Press. "And Harbaugh is on the cusp of being an iconic figure among the general population in the same demographic."

So with Harbaugh's annual salary at $7 million, he is just behind Saban and is among the nation's highest paid coaches. "It doesn't bother me he's that close to the top," Manuel said. "I think he's worth everything that we pay him, and we're happy to have him as our coach. I hope that as we all work to have success here at

Michigan that people look at what we do and say we're all worth what we're paid in that we bring that benefit. I think Jim has proven that he brings tremendous benefit to our football program, to this department, and this university. So I don't have any problems. I think he's worth every penny."

7

The Quarterback Competition

T HE BREADTH OF JIM HARBAUGH'S CONTACT LIST WAS on display earlier in 2016 during the February "Signing of the Stars" extravaganza when guests included pro wrestler Ric Flair, former Detroit Tigers manager Jim Leyland, the musicians Migos— Harbaugh would join them on stage two months later during a rap concert in Ann Arbor and pose for photos while wearing heavy gold chains and a diamond watch—former Notre Dame coach Lou Holtz, and NASCAR driver Brad Keselowski. Oh, and Tom Brady, whose return visits to his alma mater had been rare.

Harbaugh's presence in Ann Arbor clearly has increased the visibility of the Michigan program and the campus. Undoubtedly, the number of celebrities who have visited the football team and school have been on an enormous upswing since he arrived. As the Wolverines headed into the season opener against Hawaii, big names, Michael Jordan and Derek Jeter, were scheduled to share the sideline with Harbaugh and his team. How much bigger could you get than those two?

Jeter, now retired from the New York Yankees, has always been a Michigan fan and briefly was enrolled to play baseball for the Wolverines. He has always been a football fan as well and would make annual bets with late-Yankees owner George Steinbrenner, an Ohio State alum, on the Michigan-Ohio State game. Even Jeter was caught up in the Harbaugh buzz and the promise of what could be an important season for the Wolverines. He said it was difficult to see Michigan lose relevancy in football in the years before Harbaugh's arrival. "I'm the biggest fan out there," Jeter said a day before the season opener. "Yeah, I was hearing it from a lot of teammates throughout the years. When every season would start, I had a lot of optimism, and they would enjoy getting on me a little bit. Now my phone doesn't ring too much."

Because he was immersed in his baseball career, Jeter had not gotten to know Harbaugh well, but he had always admired him from afar through his playing days and then his coaching career. "Who's had success at every level?" Jeter said. "He had success as a player, he had success in the NFL, he's had success in college. Whatever he's doing other people need to start doing because he's been great for both professional and college athletics."

Jeter and Michigan football share an alliance with the Nike Jordan Brand. He was the first non-basketball athlete to be associated with the Jordan Brand and Jumpman, and Michigan was the first football program to be part of that brand. "It's huge," Jeter said. "To see now the Jumpman on the football uniforms of the University of Michigan, it's awesome. It just shows how much the brand has grown throughout the years and will continue to grow."

Michigan's season opening opponent, Hawaii, had already played its season opener—in Sydney, Australia, against Cal. The Rainbow Warriors would eventually travel nearly 50,000 miles during the 2016 season for seven road games. Hawaii coach Nick Rolovich thought he would have some fun with the Hawaii beat reporters prior to the Michigan game, but no one was really clued in on the joke until much later. Rolovich said Hawaii had requested scrimmage film from Michigan, which is unheard of. "With them not having a game and us having a game we asked if they would send us their scrimmage," the first-year Hawaii coach told reporters. "But they wouldn't. I'm sure they found our game somewhere or at least got in on TV and watched it, so they'll have a little idea what we do where there's going to be a little bit of uncertainty on our side. I guess they're trying to hide the quarterback for a reason. I think it's a little bit of [strategy] and maybe something for us to talk about, but there's enough to worry about than to really spend our time worrying about who the quarterback's going to be."

Rolovich, of course, was referring to the fact Harbaugh had not and did not plan to announce Michigan's starting quarterback until game time. Two days later while on his weekly Detroit radio appearance, Harbaugh said he had no knowledge of this story and was unaware of the scenario Rolovich had discussed. "First of all, I don't know anything about it," Harbaugh said. "I don't know anything about any request for scrimmage tape or practice tape, not aware of any request the University of Hawaii made for practice tape or scrimmage tape."

By the time Rolovich and the Rainbow Warriors had landed, the story had taken on a life of its own. He later told ESPN Radio he was not being serious. "I was actually just joking that I think it'd be fair if they sent us some practice film, some scrimmage film, I think that'd be fair, but it kind of blew up from there," Rolovich said. "There was never any real interaction or discussion of this." And he apologized for the confusion. "I mean, we're on a 10-hour plane ride, and it all happened when we were on the plane and it kind of took off from there."

Earlier in the summer Rolovich had interacted with Harbaugh when he visited Hawaii for satellite camp stops. The two worked well together, and Rolovich gained an appreciation for college football's most polarizing coach. "I think he brings some life, some extra life, to college football," Rolovich said.

While they worked the camp, Rolovich, a former college quarterback at Hawaii, said he had seen a ranking of the best college coaches as determined by their playing careers. Harbaugh, a longtime NFL veteran, was No. 1. He challenged Harbaugh to a pregame quarterback challenge before the game at Michigan Stadium and he had heard Harbaugh accepted. Rolovich jokingly said he did push-ups on the plane to stay in shape for the challenge. (For the record the quarterback challenge never transpired.)

Meanwhile, Harbaugh remained coy throughout the week as to who would be starting at quarterback, maintaining it was still an ongoing competition. He had gone the same route the year before, choosing not to name Jake Rudock as the starter until he took the field. But on the Friday before game week, the quarterbacks met the media, and of the group, Wilton Speight stood tallest—and not just because he's 6'6" and was, actually, the tallest of the quarterbacks. The redshirt sophomore carried himself differently, like a guy who knew he'd be starting the opener. He had already emerged from spring practice with a slight edge over John O'Korn and Shane Morris.

Harbaugh did reveal that he told the team who would be starting, but no one outside the team needed to know, completely keeping with Harbaugh's established style. Although he does not have a particularly adversarial relationship with the media, he is not exactly forthcoming.

Speight had been largely overlooked the first spring Harbaugh took over. He was nursing an injury and just wasn't productive. Since his sophomore year in high school in Richmond, Virginia, he worked with quarterback trainer Steve Clarkson, the self-proclaimed "Dream Maker," at least according to his website. Clarkson has worked with a number of quarterbacks, including Ben Roethlisberger and Matt Cassel, and saw Speight's talent from the moment they began working together. Where Speight stands apart, Clarkson said, is his work ethic. "He is a tireless worker," he said. "He wants to be the very, very best."

In an effort to be the very, very best he could be, Speight, an avid golfer, curtailed that summer habit. He also didn't spend much time in Richmond with his family and used his extra time in Ann Arbor watching film and throwing as much as possible. He fit in a trip to California to work with Clarkson. "I played a lot less golf," Speight said. "Two summers before when I had any free time, it was, 'Let's get out to the links.' This summer I kept the clubs in the garage and I didn't go home as much. The past two summers, I went home a lot more. They understood. I didn't want to look back at camp this time and say, 'I wish I had done more. I wish I didn't tee it up as much in June, July, or August.'"

That kind of application, that kind of devotion to the game is something Harbaugh greatly appreciates. As the season rolled on, comparisons to Roethlisberger became typical when teammates or coaches talked about Speight and his progress. But before the season opener, Clarkson was the first to draw the comparison, which he had maintained for several years—even as early as 2013 when he produced a video, *Wilton Speight The Next Big Ben*. He used film of Speight from high school and of Roethlisberger from the Pittsburgh Steelers to show the comparisons. "He's a very tall quarterback, obviously can see over the O-line, and he throws really good fade balls," senior receiver Jehu Chesson said. "In the huddle he's very vocal. He's very loud. He's very clear. I think his growth has been tremendous from the day he stepped on this campus to today."

Speight, who also played basketball and lacrosse in high school, is long limbed, which sometimes suggests a lack of mobility. But during the spring game, he proved more than capable of escaping when needed. "The thing that will surprise people considering how big he is—6'6" and 245—he's quite agile," Clarkson said. "Watch how he moves in the pocket. Pull up his high school stuff. You'll be pleasantly surprised. We call it a productive scramble. He's not panicky. He will make the plays."

Where Speight showed his growth was in terms of his leadership. When quarterbacks arrive in California to work with Clarkson, he typically asks them for one area on which they would like to focus and what they would like to improve. Although Clarkson had always considered Speight a "natural born leader," Speight thought his confidence was something on which he needed to work. "And how he carried himself," Clarkson said. "We spent time with him essentially reaffirming what he learned in spring football. I had him work a few camps for me and would carry on the playcalling and the command of the game. He focused on the nuances, what they do at Michigan, and teach that to other college quarterbacks and up-and-coming high school quarterbacks. We worked on how he carries his shoulders and to look people in the eye not look through them. When you're evaluating people, I wouldn't put it past Coach Harbaugh to study mannerisms to see how truthful they are and how genuine. I haven't seen too many people carry themselves like Wilton has, especially those who haven't yet been established as a starter. Everything he says comes out organic and authentic. That's what separates him."

That summer work paid off when Speight met the media for the first time the Friday before the first game of the season. He carried himself like the guy in charge. His shoulders were back, he looked everyone in the eye and with an air of confidence prior to the season opener.

Hawaii would try to defend Michigan's offense with its secret weapon—defensive coordinator Kevin Lempa, who had been on staff at Boston College with new Michigan defensive coordinator Don Brown. The two men had known each other for the better part of three decades and coached together five years at Maryland and Boston College.

Brown was Boston College's defensive coordinator, and Lempa coached the defensive backs for three seasons before returning to Hawaii, where he had been defensive coordinator from 2000 to 2002. "Let me tell you, he's a very creative man," Lempa said of Brown, confirming Harbaugh's hunches when he hired him. "He's really bright in what he tries to do. He tries to scheme each week and have different patterns of attack. It's hard to know where he's coming from because he changes things to fit the team he's playing. I learned a lot of techniques and a lot of scheme from being with Don for five years. He's the best defensive coordinator I've worked with. He treats the players with respect, but he gets after them. And they know he loves him. His demeanor, the way he goes about his business, I learned a lot from him."

Because Lempa had modeled his approach to defense in part from his time working with Brown, he had a feel for how Brown would coach Michigan's defense, and certainly Brown would have an idea how to help Michigan's offense prepare. But there was never any doubt that Brown would have way more defensive weapons than Lempa and the Rainbow Warriors, and the Wolverines rolled to a 63–3 season-opening victory with the heavy duty celebrity triumvirate of Michael Jordan, the game's honorary captain; Jeter; and 1997 Heisman Trophy winner, Charles Woodson, on the Michigan sideline.

Harbaugh's Wolverines opened the season ranked No. 7 and had the scheduling luxury of five straight home games, of which Hawaii was the first. Not unexpectedly, Speight started at quarterback for the Wolverines, but perhaps somewhat surprising, Harbaugh, who has never shied from playing freshmen, played 18 freshmen in the game.

Speight's first start will forever be remembered for his very first play, which he quickly forgot. He rolled right and was intercepted, but he responded admirably the next series, directing a solid 98-yard, 11-play drive for the Wolverines' first score of the season, a 12-yard pass to Grant Perry. "It wasn't the start I was imagining," Speight said. "I was rolling to our sideline anyway, so my momentum just carried right into Coach. He just grabbed me and hugged me and was kind of laughing. He was like, don't worry, we'll get it next drive. Don't sweat about that. And I was able to do that."

Harbaugh, the former quarterback and current quarterback whisperer, was fascinated to watch unfold how Speight would handle the interception and the next possession. "I wanted to see what he did on the next series," Harbaugh said. "It's very difficult for a quarterback to throw an interception on a series and then come back and lead a touchdown drive the following series. It's something I've always been fascinated in watching quarterbacks, and the really good ones can do that. They can think about, *I'm not going to make another bad mistake.* I mean, that's what some do, but good ones don't. I was just excited for that opportunity to see what he was going to do on the next drive. And to see him start the next drive on the 2-yard line, that's as much adversity as you can have for a quarterback starting a series, starting a drive, have thrown an interception on the previous drive and the very, very first throw of the game...But he responded in tremendous fashion to lead a touchdown drive, make big third-down conversion throws, to make as good a corner throw to Grant Perry as can be made. It can't be thrown any better. He had total command, and it speaks volumes and bodes really well for our team and bodes really well for his career as a quarterback to have done that, to come back off an interception and the very next drive go on a 98-yard touchdown drive. Now he knows he can do it. And now we can expect him to do it. Good for our team."

Michigan had 512 yards of total offense, including 306 rushing among 11 different ball carriers. Hawaii had 232 yards, including 81 rushing. In the first half, Hawaii had 16 carries for minus-16 yards rushing. One of the 18 freshmen who played for Michigan, running back Chris Evans scored two rushing touchdowns, and the defense scored twice on interception returns by Delano Hill and Channing Stribling. That took on more significance, considering All-American cornerback Jourdan Lewis was out with a hamstring issue along with defensive lineman Maurice Hurst, who was in uniform on the sideline but did not play.

But what seemed bigger after the game for the players was telling their stories of meeting Michael Jordan, who watched his Nike Jordan Brand—and the Jumpman logo that he made famous—on a football uniform for the first time. He was joined by Woodson, who essentially hatched the whole idea, on the sideline, and it had seemingly come full circle. The night before the game, Jordan met with the Michigan players for about 45 minutes in the Schembechler Hall team meeting room and took questions from them on a number of topics. The players were dazzled. "Everybody was like, 'Oh, man, it's MJ," fullback Khalid Hill, who had a touchdown in the opener, said. "He sat next to me, and I was freaking out."

Hill was asked if he had been nervous about meeting Jordan, but he brushed that off like it was old hat hanging out with one of the greatest athletes of all time. Then again, with the stream of famous people Harbaugh has had in the building, maybe it was actually not a big deal for the players. "It was just MJ," Hill said, laughing at how casually he said it. "It was like, wow, this is amazing, him being in the meeting room with us, sitting down with us, and talking to us and being real to us. He was keeping it real and telling us, 'Hey, this is how everything goes.' I appreciate him for that."

Of course, it was a freshman, Evans, who had the guts to ask the first question, which was about how Jordan was able to perform during The Flu Game, when he famously scored 38 points in Game 5 of the 1997 NBA Finals despite flu-like symptoms. "Like if I'm ever feeling sick, I'll watch the flu game, the whole game," Evans said, "just to see what he was going through and he was pushing hard. He told me the love for the game and his love for the teammates pushed him through that."

Evans had been ill the few weeks before the start of the season and he drew from Jordan. "Like how am I going to do this?" Evans said he asked himself. "Just pushing through it, like what he told me. I just use it on a bigger scale because Michael Jordan did it."

Center Mason Cole said it was "cool" to see Jordan and Harbaugh sharing the floor. "We just had an open conversation, asking him questions about competing and about his love for sports and his love for basketball," Cole said of Jordan. "It goes with everything Coach Harbaugh has been saying. You get so much better in sports by practicing and practicing hard, and I think Coach Harbaugh has made it like that for us. We go out and we practice hard."

Harbaugh after the game joked that his players listened more to Jordan than they do to him. "Michael Jordan said to the team

Friday night, and I think it resonated with everybody, he got good at basketball because he practiced it," Harbaugh said. "That's such a great carryover to football because you get good at football by playing football. He said if you love it, then you want to do it every day. And you want to do it as much as you can every day. He said it's like ice cream. If you love ice cream, then you're going to eat it every single day. That's what resonates with me because that's what our football team has been doing for the last month."

Chase Winovich, who many of his teammates say equals Harbaugh in terms of energy, asked Jordan if the famous story that he was cut from his high school team was true, and Jordan said it was. "He told us the story his high school coach who cut him picked him up every day at 6:00 AM to work him out and help him get better at his sport," Hill said. "That coach is why he's here today."

Before meeting Michael Jordan, guard Kyle Kalis had been starstruck once before in his life. He was a kid, and his father took him backstage at a Hank Williams Jr. concert. "I saw him, 'Bocephus, Bocephus, I'm Kyle, I'm Kyle," Kalis said, referring to Williams by the name Hank Williams Sr. had called his son and later led to the song, "My Name Is Bocephus."

He was equally starstruck meeting MJ. "When Jordan came here, I was a little girl," he said. "I was screaming to Erik [Magnuson]. We were both jumping up and down. We're in amazing positions, we're blessed to be able to meet people like that. There's not many people who can say they met Michael Jordan. I can. I'm super lucky and I think about that all the time."

Former interim athletic director Jim Hackett, who had negotiated the deal with Nike before his run as AD ended early in 2016, also attended the season opener and sported several Michigan Nike Jordan items. He modeled his new Jordan shoes, saying they are his favorite new item from the collection. The night before the game, while Jordan was speaking to the players, Hackett had dinner with former Wolverines Dan Dierdorf and Jim Brandstatter, the

Michigan radio team, and Harbaugh's parents, Jack and Jackie. He decided to send Woodson a text. "I sent him a text and said, 'I want to thank you,' because it was his idea to use Jordan," Hackett said. "He was at the very, very beginning of this. And he replied, 'Nice kicks.'"

Hackett, who had moved on to his new role with Ford, was not at the wild midnight sale at the M Den when the Nike apparel was first made available. But he did drop by a store in west Michigan where he lives and did some investigative work. "I asked the young salesperson, 'So how's the gear selling?'" Hackett said. "She said the Jordan is selling really well, but she said, 'But it's very expensive.' I said, 'It's really popular?' And she said yeah. That really made my day."

8

The Rise of the Freshmen

A BOUT MIDWAY THROUGH JIM HARBAUGH'S FIRST season at Michigan, the players made it clear they believed that based on their coach's sideline histrionics, among other less public demonstrations, he had their backs. That prompted many of them to say they would run through a brick wall for him.

At the start of Week 2, though buoyed by the team's success in the opener, Harbaugh launched into his disappointment in what ESPN analyst Ed Cunningham had said Saturday during the television broadcast about All-American cornerback Jourdan Lewis, who had missed the game with a then-undisclosed injury. But during the first half of the Hawaii game, Cunningham speculated that Lewis was out for disciplinary reasons. Harbaugh was incensed. "It had nothing to do with any off-field suspension," he said. "I heard about Ed Cunningham, got way out over his skis, speculating it was some kind of suspension. Jourdan Lewis is one of the finest guys we have on the team. Football character and off-the-field character, just total character. There's few, if any, better than Jourdan Lewis, just wanted to clarify that for the record."

The next day, Cunningham called a Michigan official to acknowledge the mistake, and though he didn't personally speak to Harbaugh, the air had been cleared. "We're good," Harbaugh said. "Sometimes we all do, we all misspeak. We're all good. And Jourdan's good."

As the Wolverines prepared for their next opponent, Central Florida, youth was being celebrated in Ann Arbor. After 18 true freshmen, including 16 on scholarship, played in the rout of Hawaii, it was more than clear that Harbaugh's "meritocracy" excludes no one. If you're a freshman and you can play, you play.

Later in the season, senior Jake Butt would talk to why that approach is so sound. It doesn't allow the veterans to get too comfortable and it allows the young players—and incoming recruits—to see evidence, plenty of evidence, that Harbaugh will play the best. "It just shows there's really no favorites. It's whoever is the best on the field will play," sophomore receiver Grant Perry said. "And that's a great thing because a lot of players want to play early and want to get that experience. I know that really helped me playing all last year. That's just a great thing he's doing. I think it really benefits the player."

Left tackle Grant Newsome got some starting time as a freshman, which generally is more unusual for an offensive lineman since they typically use their first season to get stronger and take a redshirt. But Newsome was now the starter at left tackle. Like Perry, Newsome appreciated the fact that if you're a freshmen and you want to play, you simply have to earn the playing time. "They said I should play, and I said, 'Yes, please,'" Newsome said. "It was a big boost of my confidence, knowing they were confident in me. It's great to play under a coach where you know if you're the best at your position, you're going to play. I think that's how it should be. It should be a meritocracy. A lot of programs you see, players won't start until their redshirt junior or redshirt sophomore years at the least. It's a great system where if you're the best at your position you'll play, no matter what age you are."

Harbaugh said getting the young players on the field was "tremendous for morale." "It's a meritocracy on who plays," he said. "By your effort, by your talent, you will be known."

Interestingly, though, Harbaugh has the freshmen in a separate locker room during the season. It's exactly the same as the varsity locker room—only smaller in dimension and minus a few benches. There are several reasons he chose to do this, namely the age difference between a freshman and a senior and fifth-year seniors. And he wanted the freshmen to bond and develop something lasting that will carry them through their careers as they become the senior leaders. "Honestly, I was just happy to be in a locker room at Michigan," Perry said. "I really got to know all the freshmen really well and all the walk-ons. It was cool."

Jedd Fisch, the passing game coordinator who also coaches the quarterbacks and receivers, had encouraged something he called the "buddy system," so that the sophomores sort of mentored the freshmen. Perry, for instance, said he guided three of the freshmen receivers and took Nate Johnson under his wing. "He followed me around Friday night and Saturday morning and he got a free pass to come into the varsity locker room," Perry said, laughing about Johnson's maneuvering the previous week.

Harbaugh is an interesting orator. He quotes Winston Churchill, great writers, and his father and then he will come up with things on his own. Senior defensive lineman Ryan Glasgow joked about hearing Harbaugh mention that the team's "competitive waters have been almost boiling." He said that's absolutely been true and that the message has been clear to the veterans—don't play hard and a young player, even a freshman, may take your spot.

Glasgow said if he had played as a freshman he would have had the classic "deer-in-headlights" look, but he said this group handled the opener well because of the way Harbaugh prepared them. Glasgow would later say that the freshmen recruited by Harbaugh were a good year, if not more, ahead of where he and his fellow seniors were when they came into Michigan. "When you go through a Coach Harbaugh-led football camp, you are more prepared for a football season, and I think that showed up on Saturday with the freshmen stepping in and doing a great job for the most part across the board," Glasgow said. "The coaching staff we have now is amazing at explaining concepts to all the players. I think they picked it up ridiculously fast. And nowadays, our extra summer stuff helped, going through plays with them. Senior-led workouts helped a lot; we really didn't do much of that when I was a freshman.

So top to bottom, I think we're doing a better job teaching in the program, and it's showing up on the field."

The largest freshman, offensive/defensive lineman Michael Onwenu, who was pushing 380 pounds, became quite the story after the first game. His teammates had marveled throughout preseason camp—and especially after he played snaps on both sides of the ball in Michigan's season opener against Hawaii—at his ability to move as well as he does considering his size. "Big Mike is just Big Mike," Jabrill Peppers said.

While meeting with local media for the first time, he was asked what he typically eats during the day. "I like grapes. I like fruits. I eat a lot of fruits," Onwenu said. Everyone laughed. Who could imagine that such an enormous man ate lots of grapes? "I don't even eat as much as people think I do. I don't eat a lot of junk food. Sometimes I don't feel like eating a lot of food so I'll take a little snack."

Onwenu, who had played high school football at Cass Tech, had never been a little guy, but he was always quick and athletic. "Even when I played Little League, I was the fastest big guy," he said. "Now I've gained more pounds. I still try to be as fast as I was."

His more famous fellow freshman, Rashan Gary, the No. 1 player in the country coming out of high school, had also made his debut, giving Michigan fans a hint of what his future might hold. Gary had always imagined hearing his name announced in Michigan Stadium after making his first tackle. That moment became a reality in the season opener. "Hearing my name over the announcement is one of the greatest feelings I've ever felt," Gary said. "I've never played in front of so many people. It was better than I imagined it."

Easily the most recognizable name in the freshman recruiting class, Gary said when classes began he just tried to blend in. "I'm just a normal person," he said. "I just play football. I try to stay low, but yeah, a couple people know me, say hi, and take pictures. Besides that you see me with a hoodie on."

While the freshmen had taken center stage after the season

opener, Wilton Speight was a main focus and would be going forward. Before the season-opening start, his most significant playing time had come the previous season late in the game at Minnesota when starting quarterback Jake Rudock was sidelined with an injury. Michigan was trailing, the game was on the line, and Speight, the backup, had to take over.

He shrugged off a shaky first series and then led Michigan to the go-ahead touchdown, a 12-yard pass to Jehu Chesson with less than five minutes left. The defense's goal-line stop preserved the win, but Speight was the one who directed the scoring drive. That moment, to those who had worked with Speight, is when he elevated his confidence and level of play. "When you're the No. 2, you have to prepare as the No. 1," Fisch said during UCF week. "The reality check came when he went into the game and we weren't winning. And then you really realize not only are you one play away from going into the game, you're one play away from having to win the game. I think that really helped him."

That, in addition to his summer work with Steve Clarkson, might have given Speight the edge he needed entering the quarterback competition in the spring and then into the fall camp.

After Michigan's 63–3 victory against Hawaii, Speight said Harbaugh laughed off his first-play interception during the game. That's exactly how Fisch said they operate—keep undo pressure off the players during games, which is why Harbaugh and his staff aren't seen yelling at players on the sideline. "Kind of the school I was from, you coach them as hard as you want Sunday through Friday and then on Saturday you've got to be their advocate on gameday," Fisch said. "To second-guess and question things on gameday and be overly critical on gameday, I don't know what the value is. I think Sunday we go into the film review and make all the corrections. Our job at that point is to support him and give him the best chance to succeed."

Fisch said Speight continued to build on his confidence as his workload increased in the spring and preseason camp. "He's had a big jump. There's no question about that at this point in time. Going into the Game 1 of last year, I think he only had 75 reps in camp," Fisch said. "It's a huge jump, and I give him a lot of credit for it. He gained confidence in the game he went in. The second half of training camp of last year, he continued to improve. It's a different Wilton nowadays. It's definitely a more confident guy."

Glasgow and Speight are roommates, and Glasgow had seen the changes. "I've seen him mature a lot since he came here," Glasgow said. "I've seen him grow up very significantly since spring ball to now, especially since last spring ball when Coach Harbaugh first got here. Coach Harbaugh did a pretty good job rattling Wilton's cage when he first got here. I don't think the quarterbacks had ever been coached as hard as Coach Harbaugh coaches them. [Speight has] adapted to it and taken everything in stride, and I'm really proud of how far he's come."

Clarkson clearly had also helped Speight take another step toward becoming a starter. College quarterback coaches don't always like the idea of their quarterbacks working with an "outsider"— former UM offensive coordinator/quarterbacks coach Al Borges was against it—but Fisch endorsed the extra work. "There's some value there," Fisch said. "I've been around quarterbacks that have really flourished by having a guy they can go back home to or have somebody who can work or tweak a mechanic, something they've seen since seventh grade or eighth grade that they can see a certain development they can help with."

And with that added help, Speight won the job in what Fisch described as a close competition. "It went down to the end," Fisch said. "The way I described it to the quarterbacks, Wilton kind of had the pole position after spring. He had a little bit of an edge. The race started, and the green flag was waved, and people were trying to pass people, and he kind of never got passed. He continued to play better."

Michigan improved two spots in the Associated Press poll heading into the game against Central Florida and its spread offense. The Wolverines struggled to run the ball against a defense that loaded the box, but fullback Khalid Hill, receiver Amara Darboh, and tight end Jake Butt each scored two touchdowns. The Wolverines blocked four first-half kicks, including two field goals, and Speight was 25-of-37 for 312 yards, four touchdowns, and zero interceptions in a 51–14 victory.

Central Florida coach Scott Frost, despite seeing his team lose by a lopsided margin, said his team "outhit" Michigan throughout the game. "It's hard to say when the score is what it is, but we came in here and outhit those guys today," Frost told reporters after the game. "Standing on the sideline, there's no doubt which team was hitting harder. Our guys came in hungry and wanted to do that. It's rare you can come into Michigan and rush for 300 yards on them. They had to run a fly sweep in the fourth quarter to get to 100. I give our defense a ton of credit."

He said he expected a physical game from the Wolverines because that's how Harbaugh coaches. "Jim Harbaugh teams are physical," Frost said. "That's what he's known for. We came in and rushed for six yards a carry; they had 2.9. That tells me our guys are playing hard."

Earlier in the year, after Harbaugh hosted the star-studded "Signing of the Stars," Frost opened his Signing Day news conference saying, "As long as I'm running this program, we're not going to make a zoo out of National Signing Day." When Frost appeared on the *Open Mike* radio show in Orlando, Florida, the next day, he was asked why he felt the need to make that comment. "Recruiting has become a circus," Frost said. "Long-term I don't want to recruit a lot of guys here who are going to wait until the last day to put four or five hats on a table and hold teams hostage to wait and see what they're going to do. I want kids who want to be at UCF, not kids who want to be recruited. It's great to get the attention. It's great that people are interested. Obviously, college football is a product everybody wants to be a part of and is excited about. But, to be honest with you, it's tough on kids. For a year or two as they're being recruited, these young men have everybody from Rivals to Scout to ESPN to local media to coaches telling them how great they are. The kids who fall in love with that process and start believing the hype, it's a tougher transition for them."

After hearing about Frost's postgame comments, Harbaugh took the high road as he disagreed. "They hit well," Harbaugh said. "That was a good, physical football team, and I was impressed with the way they tackled, I was impressed with the way they played. I was very impressed with their speed. I agree, they played very well. My view of it after the game and after watching the film was that we got the job done. We took care of business physically in the lines. I feel the same as I did after the game."

Michigan was held to 119 rushing yards on 41 attempts, as the backs were unable to find holes against a stacked line that opted to dare Speight to throw. Central Florida had some big plays on the Michigan defense, including three quarterback scrambles. UCF had five big plays that accounted for 212 of 275 rushing yards on 46 attempts. "You'll notice I didn't say we dominated," Harbaugh said. "But I thought we got the better of it. We got the better of it. Not by a huge margin. They have a very good football team, they're very well-coached. I was impressed with their aggression, their toughness, and their speed."

And with that Harbaugh wished UCF luck the rest of the season and moved on. Before Harbaugh could move on to Week 3, though, he felt compelled to address a subject that had taken social media by storm during the Michigan-UCF game—he allegedly picked his nose and then put his finger in his mouth. A video clip from television made the Internet rounds. Because it was Harbaugh, it became a big deal.

So big a deal that on his weekly radio show, Harbaugh decided to clear the air. When asked if he wanted to address anything, he tried to close the book on the "controversy" in a very good-natured manner. "I have never eaten a booger in my entire life," Harbaugh said. "It might have looked like that was happening. But if you rub your nose and then you bite your fingernail, that's not eating a booger. There was no booger eaten."

And once more for emphasis. "For clarity here, for the record, I have never eaten a booger in my entire life."

It did not end there. BoogerGate was kept alive by Harbaugh's brother, John, who took time at the start of his weekly conference call with the opposing team's media (in this instance Cleveland) and felt compelled to also claim his younger brother's innocence. "Can I say something for the record, since this Cleveland?" John Harbaugh asked the media. "My brother has never eaten a booger."

John admitted there was enough evidence to prove there was contact between his brother's finger an nose. "[But] nothing came out," John Harbaugh said before adding the fact he has never been guilty of eating a booger either. This was the moment you just shake your head and think, *Only Jim Harbaugh.*

9

Legends Return to Ann Arbor

F REDDY P. SOFT IS STEEPED IN THE CREATIVE
background of Jack Harbaugh and was given new life by his son,
Jim. Freddy P. Soft had made appearances in conversations when
Harbaugh was coaching the San Francisco 49ers and had been part
of Harbaugh's summer time speeches to youth campers. Mr. Soft
is an imaginary character Harbaugh used as a way to help young
athletes understand the signs of some inner being who wanted to
undermine growth, progress, and the fulfillment of personal goals.

If you dissect any athlete in any sport, he or she will tell of
doubts deep in training for whatever event or endeavor. In the 1970s
the book *The Inner Game of Tennis* described the mental side of
peak performance and that there are often two voices in your head
identified as Self 1 and Self 2. Freddy P. Soft essentially is Harbaugh's
version of that negative self, the one that strives to create self-doubt
and destroy goals. He is that little devil on your shoulder telling you
to take it easy, relax, instead of working harder to get better.

As Michigan opened practice the week of the Colorado game
in September, Harbaugh was asked at his Monday news conference
about fictional Freddy P. Soft and he easily launched into a
description of the invented character. "He's a four-inch guy that
wears a cape and a hat with a plume in it," Harbaugh said, animatedly. "He's just tall enough to talk right into your ear and tell you,
'You don't have to practice today. Why are you working so hard?
Get over there in the shade. No need to attack with enthusiasm
unknown to mankind today. So take a break. Take a knee.' He's not
a guy you want around. You want to get him off your shoulders fast
as possible."

Harbaugh had introduced the concept of Freddy P. Soft to

his players when he coached the 49ers. A story on SFGate.com in 2011 indicated that "Watch out for Freddy" was a team mantra. *The Sacramento Bee* even ran a humorous Q&A story with Freddy. Harbaugh was visibly delighted to revive conversation about Freddy P. Soft, who he said, has aliases like Frederick P. Soft and Mr. Soft. But whatever the name, he apparently had come around Michigan practices every once in a while. And everyone is in on Freddy P. Soft.

Quarterback Wilton Speight said that offensive coordinator Tim Drevno, who of the Michigan assistants has had the longest working relationship with Harbaugh, will yell at the imaginary motivational device. The long, arduous preseason practices are fertile ground for Mr. Soft. And although it is a way to keep players focused, they have fun with it, too. "Coach Drevno kind of brought Freddy P. Soft, a little guy, Freddy P. Soft sitting on the shoulder, and we love when he brings it out because Coach Drevno starts yelling at Freddy P. Soft saying, 'Get out of here,'" Speight said. "It's the funniest thing ever. All you've got to do is flick Freddy P. Soft out of there, and you'll be good to go."

Like many things Harbaugh generated, the Freddy P. Soft conversation reached a national level and became a hot topic on SiriusXM's college sports station. Former college coach Rick Neuheisel, who knows Harbaugh from their coaching days in the Pac-12 when Harbaugh was at Stanford and Neuheisel at UCLA, is musically inclined. While on the show, he often brings out his guitar and sings. That week Neuheisel had gone for a walk and was thinking about the fictional character and figured he needed to be immortalized in song. "That is too good," Neuheisel told himself. "Freddy P. Soft—that's got to be a song." He decided to pay tribute to the four-inch trouble-maker and sang his version of the famous "King of the Road" and changed it to "Freddy P. Soft."

It was an interesting start to Colorado week that had so many storylines weaving throughout. Tom Brady, the former Wolverine and current Super Bowl champion, would serve as the Michigan honorary captain. A Brady appearance in Ann Arbor has always been a big deal. Then there was the fact the last time Colorado played at Michigan Stadium was in 1994 and featured the Hail Mary heard around the world. Diagnosed with late-onset dementia, former Colorado coach Bill McCartney, also a former beloved Michigan assistant under Bo Schembechler, would be returning to be honored before and during the game, and the Colorado sports information staff would have some fun with the fact Michigan doesn't issue a depth chart. Except Harbaugh didn't find it that funny.

But the Wolverines, who had outscored their first two opponents 114–17, had quickly moved three spots to No. 4 in the AP top 25 poll. Most coaches tell their players not to pay attention to rankings. Not Harbaugh. He has said repeatedly over his coaching and playing career that there are trophies, both academic and athletic, that they should all strive to win. Even if it's something subjective—like a poll voted on by writers—they should care about it and want to win and be at the top.

The Michigan players seemed to enjoy this new take on poll watching. "Coach Harbaugh talked to us the other day before the game about now we're getting ranked up there, we're No. 4 or whatever, and a lot of guys might say, 'You know, the rankings don't mean anything. We don't care about the rankings,'" senior offensive lineman Kyle Kalis said after a practice. "But no, we care about the rankings. We wanted to be the highest ranked we can possibly be. That's the expectation."

Tight end Ian Bunting said their approach to the rankings was to set them as another goal. "Why wouldn't you pay attention to it?" Bunting said. "You should embrace that and use that as motivation to work even harder because you know everyone is coming for you."

What Harbaugh wasn't paying attention to, however, was Colorado's clever depth chart that became an Internet sensation and featured a Who's Who in the entertainment world. Traditionally before each game, a package of game notes is provided to the media, and those notes include a depth chart. Michigan, though, was going to go depth-chart free, a decision made by Harbaugh before the season.

In an effort to lighten up things and have fun with the fact Harbaugh wasn't providing a depth chart, Colorado sports information director David Plati gave the Buffaloes' depth chart a facelift. According to that depth chart, the offense was to run a Single Wing-T, and the defense would be in the 4-0-7. Elmer Fudd, a 5'2", 165-pound senior, was at quarterback, while leading the defense was James Bond—with the very appropriate jersey No. 007. Happy Gilmore was the punter. The three hockey Hanson brothers, Steve, Jack, and Jeff, were the halfbacks, and one-fourth back was Billy Ray Valentine.

Michigan's players thought it was funny.

Harbaugh didn't.

During his weekly Detroit radio appearance, Harbaugh was jokingly asked about facing Elmer Fudd. "That was interesting, as well," Harbaugh said, sounding unamused. "In our preparation for Colorado, we've had a hard time working humor into the preparations. They're a very good football team."

Michigan and Colorado had a humorous back and forth on Twitter after the depth chart was released. Harbaugh had not read those exchanges, but he saw the depth chart. "I was trying to imagine how many people sat around and how many hours they worked on that," he said. "We've just found when it comes to the depth chart, modern technology seems to have made the depth chart to be an outdated task by about 20 years. We find studying last week's film of the opponent is the most accurate way of determining another team's depth chart."

Harbaugh said the media does not need a depth chart. "There's so much written about the team that's on the Internet," Harbaugh said. "For those of us who watch the games, [we] just felt modern technology is the most accurate way of studying and knowing what the opponent's depth chart and who's playing in the game is to look at the previous week's film and not rely on another PR director's assessment of what the depth chart is. You just go right to the tape."

Maybe Colorado was trying to poke the bear, maybe it wasn't, but things didn't end with the depth chart. The Buffaloes decided to go old school with their uniform and would wear the same uniform the 1994 team wore when they beat Michigan on the Hail Mary. For those who are asked to list some of the more memorable games in the history of Michigan Stadium, that 1994 game is always included because of the stunning fashion of the loss. It really was a moment burned in the memory of those who played the game, those who were there, and those who watched or listened.

For years Michigan fans would tell former linebacker Steve Morrison their story about that game. He's heard from those who left early—confident the Wolverines' 26–21 lead was solid. He's heard the horror stories from those who stayed and watched as Michigan allowed two Colorado scores in the final 2:16 of the game, including *The Play*. He has a pretty standard response. "My angle was a lot worse than yours, so don't even try it," Morrison, a former college coach now living in Ann Arbor, said. "It's never going to go away. It was absolute disbelief. Every time I see it, it's almost out-of-body-like now. *No, that can't be me.* But it is. I tell people who ask if I was there, 'Yeah, I was there. Just watch the end of the game when they pan to the player with his hands on his helmet.'"

As soon as Michael Westbrook caught the amazing throw from Kordell Stewart on the final play that began with six seconds left to win the game 27–26, Morrison struck that pose with his hands on his helmet in absolute disbelief. "It was shock," Morrison said. Throughout his coaching career, Morrison had been on both sides of that type of play. "It's just that our heartbreak was in front of 100,000 people," he said. "Let's face it. It makes the game great in a way because there's always an opportunity to make plays." The hurt has never left, and he suspects it never will. But Morrison has another perspective. "As much as I hated being part of it, now I can think there's a beauty to that play," Morrison said. "The way he threw that football...time stood still."

Tyrone Wheatley, the former Michigan running back who joined Harbaugh's staff to coach running backs, was coming off an injury and was limited in that game. The week of this game, he made it clear he was not keen on revisiting that game. "Because I was there and I was on the sideline and thought we had the game won, and to have a Detroit native [Westbrook] come in the freaking building and steal one from us and go back to Colorado wasn't a great feeling," Wheatley said. "Certain things you carry with you, and it sticks with you. I didn't play that much in that game. You're like, 'Man, if I was healthy, maybe I could have helped a little bit.' It's still a bad feeling."

Wheatley could not watch Stewart on that final play and turned around. "And then it was silent, and then everybody was like, 'Ohhhhh, man,'" he said. "At that point in time, the stands were almost empty, and there was a brief moment of silence, and then it was, 'I can't believe it, I can't believe it.' I looked up, and [the Buffaloes] were running around, and it was like, 'You've got to be kidding me.' That was a tough one. That was a tough one. Stewart threw the heck out of the ball, though."

The coach of that Colorado team, McCartney returned that week as the Buffaloes' honorary captain and would be feted the night before by many of his former players at Michigan.

McCartney had been on staff along with Jack Harbaugh, so Jim Harbaugh had fond memories of the coach and his family. And their cereal options. "Great family, love the McCartneys," Harbaugh said. "They had the best cereal of anybody in the neighborhood. We had Cheerios. No flavor. You go to the McCartneys, and they had one of those carousels in the cabinet with Cap'n Crunch and Lucky Charms and Froot Loops. A wide assortment, 10 or 12 different kinds of really good cereal. Lyndi [McCartney's late wife] was great.

If you were hungry, you could just come in and get yourself a bowl of cereal."

McCartney, a native of Riverview, just outside of Detroit, went on to lead Colorado to a national championship and was a leader, an expert motivator, and a terrific communicator.

For those who were recruited by or played for him at Michigan while he was an assistant from 1974 to 1981 on Bo Schembechler's staff, McCartney made an unforgettable impact. "Mac was just a special guy, a special coach," former Michigan quarterback John Wangler said. "You talk about certain guys coming through your life who leave a great impression and who change your life and who you have the highest respect for, Mac's one of those guys. Anyone he touches, they remember."

His family had recently announced that McCartney, 76, was diagnosed with late-onset Alzheimer's disease, and the College Football Hall of Fame coach mostly has issues with short-term memory. A large number of former Michigan players, who were recruited and coached by McCartney, attended a reception for him the night before the game, and they wore T-shirts that read: "Thanks Coach Mac." About 50 former Colorado players also attended. "He believed in the holistic development of his students and grounded in core values," Boston College athletic director Brad Bates, who played defense at Michigan under McCartney, said. "I studied how he communicates. He was a genius communicator, and his ability to inspire and motivate was amazing. I learned so much on a communication level from him."

And while McCartney was Colorado's honorary captain, Brady would serve as Michigan's honorary captain since he was serving a four-game NFL suspension. Before every game Harbaugh throws with the quarterbacks. He likes to do it, he can still throw, and he gets a firsthand look at how the quarterbacks are performing. But there on the field before the Colorado game, Harbaugh and Brady, two former Michigan quarterbacks, played catch. But more on that later. There was a game to play, and for the Wolverines, who had outscored their opponents 114–17 the previous two weeks, suddenly and very quickly were in unfamiliar territory down two touchdowns at the end of the first quarter against the Buffaloes.

But the Wolverines, who said it was good to experience some early adversity, particularly after the routs of their first two games, outscored the Buffaloes 38–7 during the last three quarters to win 45–28. "I really do think we did [need this game] because it's only going to get tougher from here," tight end Jake Butt said. "Honestly, this was not our best week of practice. It really wasn't. One thing we stress all the time, you're going to play how you practice and how you prepare. We found a way to get it done. We can look back and learn from this. If we want to be the best team in the country or one of the best teams in the country, we've got to practice like it, we've got to play like it, we've got to prepare like it and execute like it. It wasn't pretty. It wasn't our best game by any means. It was good enough to get the job done, though. Thankfully, we can go back and make the corrections knowing we won this game."

Michigan's do-everything Jabrill Peppers was the key spark the entire game and made important defensive stops early, giving quarterback Wilton Speight and the offense time to eventually find their way. He delivered outstanding field position off his returns and added a punt return for a touchdown late to tack an exclamation point on the victory. Peppers accounted for 204 total yards, including 99 yards on punt returns. He scored on a 54-yard punt return—the first of his career—for the Wolverines' final score. "It was definitely a sense of relief," Peppers said. "I felt a couple of those punts I could have taken one back. When you get a line drive and great blocking, man, if you don't score then, they've got to put somebody else back there. The hole was wide open. They leave it upon me to make a couple guys miss. I felt as though I did that. I started cramping about the 5. I was like, 'There's no way I'm not getting in this time.' I was tired of just being the 'almost kind of guy.'

It definitely felt good to finally punch one in."

Peppers also made his first appearance of the season on offense and had 24 yards rushing. His work, of course, was not only on special teams and offense, but also on defense. He had nine tackles, a sack, and 3.5 tackles for loss, including a one-yard loss in the first half that held the Buffaloes to a field-goal attempt they missed. "Jabrill Peppers proved he was the best player in today's game," Harbaugh said. "We don't win that game without Jabrill Peppers."

Peppers' 55-yard kickoff return in the second half gave Michigan the ball at the Buffaloes' 45-yard line and set up the Wolverines' go-ahead score to make it 31–28. They never trailed again. Rebounding from that deficit and holding it together after Colorado took a 28–24 lead early in the second half was just what the Wolverines needed, the players said. "We weren't worried," Butt said. "We knew the first two games we were really never punched in the face. Everything was going so smoothly. It's not going to be a fairy tale the whole entire season. There's going to come a point in time we were going to get punched in the face, where we were going to get backed in the corner. We fought back. We stuck together and rode that wave."

So back to that pregame game of catch with Tom Brady—even Harbaugh was dazzled.

In fact, after the game, Harbaugh was giddy. "I look back at my career of playing catch with different people. That was right there with my dad, playing catch with my dad," Harbaugh said, effusively. "Tom's got a good arm, by the way. He can rip it. He can throw it well. I wish I wouldn't have given him the wind."

Harbaugh was asked if he was competing with Brady. "Yeah, of course," Harbaugh said as he erupted in laughter. "'Let's play a little catch, Tom.' He throws a good ball. That ball almost catches itself the way he throws. That's one heck of a ball he throws."

Brady spoke to the Wolverines before the game. It was similar to how the players had met with Michael Jordan the night before the game a few weeks before. "His pregame talk was outstanding," Harbaugh said of Brady. "It was very from the heart. He went through each position, told them what was expected of them to play as the best players at their position had played through the years. It was a great message.

Butt said he shook hands with Brady in the locker room before the game. "You could feel his presence and you could look in his eyes and you could tell the way he carries himself is why he's one of the greatest of all time," Butt said. "It's special. It's special to be a captain here, and already the lineup we've had with honorary captains going on—it just shows why Michigan is such a great place."

A week later while on *The Dan Patrick Show*, Harbaugh raved about Brady's pregame words and the impact he made on the team. "The way he interacted with our players and our students and with the crowd and the way they treated him, it was special. It was a special day for Michigan football," Harbaugh said. "It was pregame talk that you would expect from Tom Brady. The paint was peeling from inside the walls of the locker room. It resonated with them. It was one of the better pregame speeches I've ever heard a coach or player tell. It was from the heart and it was exactly what they needed to hear."

10

Milk Man

I F YOU'VE LISTENED TO JIM HARBAUGH ENOUGH, YOU learn that milk plays a major role in his life. Always has. He has told little kids who have asked how to get bigger and stronger—and he has made it clear to adults—that the secret to his success was drinking milk. As he has said on multiple occasions, it's all about the whole milk, "not the candy-ass 2 percent or skim milk."

When his players have been ill, he has half-jokingly suggested they should "do more push-ups, drink more whole milk, and use hand sanitizer to improve their health and avoid further illness." This is the same man who, during his first season, offered vital Halloween strategy to youngsters, suggesting they make two costumes "to be go-getters," and by running from house to house in one costume and then changing into the other and hustling, "you can get more candy than anybody else."

It's all about the hustle for Harbaugh and very clearly all about the milk. On one of his weekly Monday night radio shows during his first season at Michigan, a fan wanted to know how his not-yet-born baby could grow to 6'5" and play quarterback at Michigan. Harbaugh shared his method to achieve everything. "I truly believe the No. 1 natural steroid is sleep, and the No. 2 natural steroid is milk, whole milk, and three would be water, and four would be steak. Eat steak," he told the Pizza House crowd. "I take a vitamin every day—it's called a steak."

That was a line borrowed from Robert Duvall's character, Buck Weston, in the 2005 movie, *Kicking & Screaming*, but it certainly sounded like vintage Harbaugh. So not surprisingly, with his team 3–0 and preparing to open Big Ten play against Penn State at Michigan Stadium in Week 4, milk became a pretty big issue. He and wife, Sarah, appeared in a humorous online digital commercial for Fairlife Milk. With the ad released on Tuesday of game week, Harbaugh made the national radio rounds to promote the brand.

Sarah, who at the time of taping was pregnant with the couple's fourth child, Harbaugh, and their three kids were featured in the ad. Sitting on a couch, Jim appears to be enthusiastically watching game film. Instead, he's watching their three children building a goal post. "A strong offensive line of calcium and proteins makes stronger bones, which means more production from the kids," Harbaugh tells his wife in the ad. "That's how we roll!"

In a moment perhaps close to reality, Harbaugh later shows in the ad he can still fit in his football pads while telling his wife he is "Captain Completion." "Less sugar means Captain Completion here can fit back into his old armor," Harbaugh said, pounding a fist on his chest. "Still fits. One team, one dream, baby."

While Harbaugh appeared on *The Dan Patrick Show* to discuss the Fairlife ad and campaign, Patrick joked that Ohio State coach Urban Meyer's milk choices are different than Harbaugh's. "Urban drinks 1 percent, by the way," Patrick said. Harbaugh played along. "Well, we refuse to drink the candy-ass skim milk or the 1 percent," he said. "We won't have any of that."

Michigan running backs Ty Isaac and De'Veon Smith watched Harbaugh's ad and got a good laugh. "It was funny," Isaac said. "The only reason we thought it was funny is because it sounded very genuine. If it wasn't scripted, I would believe it." They referenced his commentary on "candy-ass milk." "I don't drink the skim milk, so I know I'm on his good side," Isaac said.

When Harbaugh makes the national radio rounds, as he did in support of the ad, he often fields questions on a number of subjects not related to the current season. Harbaugh is such a fascinating personality that radio hosts choose to delve into other topics like the NFL, especially since he had coached the San Francisco 49ers and his brother coaches the Baltimore Ravens. And also because Jim

Harbaugh-returning-to-the-NFL will be a ceaseless undercurrent. He will play along to an extent and sometimes will even add some of his own revelations that come out of left field.

Harbaugh told Rich Eisen, a Michigan alum, on Eisen's popular podcast that while he watches Michigan tape on Sundays, he has NFL games on. He always watches the Ravens to check on big brother John. "I love watching the games," Harbaugh said.

Eisen then poked around about his NFL desires. "You don't miss any of it, do you, Coach? You don't miss it, right?" Eisen asked.

Harbaugh cleverly sidestepped. "It's still there, Rich, I don't have to miss it," Harbaugh said. "The NFL is still there. I get to watch it."

"I'm just making sure," Eisen said, speaking as a Michigan fan.

The NFL remains important to Harbaugh because, as he told Eisen, he is very much interested in developing the current Michigan players for NFL futures. "I want to get our guys there, too," Harbaugh said. "I think we're going to have quite a few players on this ballclub right now playing on Sundays next year. And into the future we have some good young players. That's a goal for them. I want that to be a goal for them. I want to see them playing at the highest level in the National Football League. I take a lot of pleasure and consider that part of my job to put our players in the position to play in the NFL."

Later on the national radio circuit, Harbaugh cut a bit loose. Appearing on *Tiki and Tierney*, Harbaugh decided to share some personal news. He has a new sleep aid, which assists those with sleep apnea. "As far as going to bed at night, I'm going to blow your whole image that you have here. I wear a sleep mask now," Harbaugh said. And he started laughing. "Let me tell you, it is good. I sleep so much better. It keeps me from dying. I'm all for it."

As much as milk is part of Harbaugh's reality, so is toughness. He appreciates that quality on a variety of levels. And as he delved into Michigan's preparations for the Wolverines' Big Ten opener, he focused on quarterback Wilton Speight, who was slammed down during their second series the previous week against Colorado. It was on a sack that generated a fumble and led to a touchdown that put Michigan in a 14–0 hole. But at that moment, Speight earned Harbaugh's respect.

A year earlier Harbaugh had described Michigan quarterback Jake Rudock as "tough as a $2 steak." That is a badge of honor for any quarterback Harbaugh coaches. Speight earned it in Week 3. "I've thought it was a true sign of somebody's character that they don't just cry victim when they're victimized," Harbaugh said on his radio show. "And he was victimized on that play. That was a shot. He didn't get up grabbing body parts and limping around. He was real tough, and it was a real opportunity for him, starting his third ballgame, to show the team that he could take a hit and get right back up. I was really impressed. That was another rung that he climbed up to on the ladder. It was impressive to guys on our football team as well."

Speight suffered an elbow injury on that hit, which probably was part of the reason he didn't look as sharp as he had the previous two games. But he did plenty that Harbaugh likes and values from his quarterback. "He played a tough, gritty ballgame and did some things with people. They kept coming in his face the entire game. He didn't flinch," Harbaugh said. "There were three, four times after that where there were people right in his face and running on the quarterback, and he sidestepped them and avoided the sack and turned it into some big plays. You know what? He played a gritty ballgame. That's something he proved to his teammates and his coach, that he's got some gravel in his guts. So I'm very impressed by that."

Michigan fans always seem to be curious with how happy Harbaugh is back in Ann Arbor. So on the radio show, he was asked the best thing about being back. "The absolute best thing is taking my two girls to school," Harbaugh said. "They go over to St. Francis [of Assisi] elementary. I get to drop them off every morning, and it's the same school that I went to. It's an awesome school. It's a clean, old Catholic school off of Stadium and across from Tappan Junior High School." In those few minutes, Harbaugh gets to be a normal parent. "They do a line so I get to stand there in line with them until the teacher comes and they walk inside," he said. "Yeah, I get to be a dad."

After an early week filled with discussions of milk and parenting, Harbaugh and the Wolverines pressed on in an effort to improve to 4–0 while facing Penn State in the Big Ten opener. All-American Jourdan Lewis, who had not played the first three games of the season, and defensive lineman Taco Charlton, who suffered an ankle injury in the season opener and had been out, were expected to return to the lineup. Harbaugh had been upbeat at his Monday news conference about their status and sounded hopeful later in the week on his Detroit radio appearance. "God willing and the creek don't rise, we'll get Jourdan back, get Taco back," Harbaugh said. "All goes well, they'll be playing. You like to see how they feel the next day, what kind of soreness they have, or how it is a day after the practice. We don't know that. We're hopeful."

Jabrill Peppers, who the previous year hadn't been introduced as an offensive threat until midway through the season, was already contributing on offense through the first three weeks. Could the do-everything Peppers possibly be able to play every play in a game? "He might," Harbaugh said. "He might be able to play every play, especially with all the TV timeouts, maybe it's possible."

Harbaugh said he tried to have a ballpark figure for how many snaps Peppers should play each game. In the Colorado game the week before, Peppers appeared on offense for the first time of the season and had two carries for 24 yards. He returned a 54-yard punt for a touchdown and was leading the country in tackles for loss. "Common sense tells you, you do," Harbaugh said about what the right play count should be. "Experience says that you do and should, but he's special. He defies common sense. He defies logic at times."

Harbaugh, who had spoken so highly of Peppers during the Big

Ten Media Days in Chicago, was starting to talk even more about how special a player he is. He singled out one of Peppers' defensive plays in the Colorado game as an example of his instincts, his athleticism, and his sheer closing speed. "It was a big hit in the game, a tackle for a loss," Harbaugh said. "He was defending a bubble screen, but when you looked at the tape, he was about 12 to 13 yards away from the receiver when their slot caught a bubble screen behind the line of scrimmage. And a lot of players will just read and react and try to get the right tackling angle. He just shot out of a canon. He ran a .7/13-yard dash right at the slot receiver. And he got there so fast before the receiver was able to get into an athletic position and make a move. He had covered 13 yards and made that tackle in the backfield. That was defying logic. It's not hyperbole. He does defy what you know, what usual football players can do, maybe that's the way to say it."

Peppers could not be relied on to do everything, though. Both Michigan's defense and run game were being questioned. But in the Big Ten opener, the Wolverines seemed to find answers in a 49–10 dismantling of Penn State. "There was improvement," Harbaugh said, praising the team for a "heck of a good" victory. "I thought our line was good [on] both sides, the quarterback, the running backs, the secondary. A lot of good football being played, has to be an A++ day."

The only negative, as Harbaugh pointed out, was cornerback Jeremy Clark tearing his anterior cruciate ligament. He suffered the season-ending knee injury with about 11 minutes left in the game, and the Michigan players gathered around him on the field as he was being evaluated before being moved to a cart. Lewis said he shed tears for Clark. "That's got everyone in the locker room a little sad right now," Harbaugh said.

The Nittany Lions were held scoreless until two long drives in the second half produced 10 points, while the Wolverines produced in every aspect. The run game, which had taken some heat the last few weeks, was dominant and averaged 6.7 yards a carry against a Penn State defense that had grown incredibly thin at linebacker. Five backs scored. Karan Higdon scored two rushing touchdowns, while Isaac, Smith, Chris Evans, and fullback Khalid Hill each had a touchdown run. Michigan had a whopping 326 yards rushing.

Since Harbaugh appreciates winning every trophy, Michigan did claim another with the Big Ten-opening victory. It entered the game leading the nation in all-time wins with 928 but trailed rival Notre Dame in winning percentage. That changed after Michigan defeated Penn State 49–10, and Notre Dame lost to Duke to fall to 1–3. The Wolverines improved to 929–331–36 with a .7307 winning percentage while Notre Dame dropped a hair to 893–316–42 or .7306.

What Harbaugh and his offensive staff also were showing in the first four games of the season was prolific scoring. Michigan scored 63 in a season-opening victory against Hawaii, 51 against Central Florida, 45 against Colorado, and 49 against Penn State, and the last time a Michigan team had scored 40 or more points in each of its first four games was 1947. (For the record, in 1947 Michigan scored 55 points, 49, 69, and 49 in the first four games.) How much of an improvement was the offense showing early in Harbaugh's second season? The Wolverines had four games scoring 40 points or more over the 25-game span of the previous two seasons combined.

Harbaugh runs a power offense and he strives for balance. Although the first four games didn't feature completely balanced run-pass offenses—since, for instance, UCF had set out to completely stuff the run—the Penn State game was about giving Michigan's running backs a chance to shine and gain confidence. By the nature of a run game, it also gave Michigan's offensive line a much-needed confidence boost as well. "We saw a big opportunity to be able to slash them in the run game," Speight said. "The offensive linemen were so happy about that. They came out with the mind-set they were going to beat their guy and win the war of the trenches."

So confident was Michigan with its run game that at one point in the second half, the Wolverines ran the same play multiple times in a row. "We'd just flip it back and forth, and I started laughing looking at the play call because they do the same signal, same number in every time," Speight said. "The linemen were getting so excited because I called the same play. I think we were getting nine or 10 [yards] a pop. When that happens it's demoralizing for a defense. I've never played defense, but I can imagine that would suck to go through that every single play, to have someone run you over. That builds our confidence and probably makes them lose confidence."

Speight looked like he was no longer having issues with the right elbow of his throwing arm that had been injured the previous week against Colorado. He did not take a sack in large part because of his ability to get out of pressure, that Roethlisberger ability that his private quarterback coach, Steve Clarkson, had talked about. Before the end of the first half, Speight kept alive a touchdown-scoring drive by scrambling nine yards to convert a fourth and long. "That hit last week I took kind of dictated the internal clock I had for the rest of the game," Speight said. "I didn't want that to carry over into this game, so I wanted to hang in the pocket as long as I could. When the opportunity was there, I knew I needed to make plays with my feet and I was able to do that."

Defensively, Michigan smothered the run. The Nittany Lions had 70 yards rushing, and talented lead back Saquon Barkley, who would go on to become the Big Ten's Offensive Player of the Year, had 59 yards on 15 carries. He also had 77 yards on five receptions. The Wolverines had 13 tackles for loss and six sacks of Penn State quarterback Trace McSorley.

Perhaps most significant for Michigan's defense was the return of Lewis, who knew it would take some time to get acclimated, but by the end of the game, he felt like he was back in game rhythm. Lewis missed the first three games of the season because of a back strain that caused issues with his hamstrings and quads from what defensive backs coach Mike Zordich said was overwork during summer workouts. "He worked his tail off all summer, probably worked a little too hard," Zordich said. "That might have been a little too much torque on his body."

Harbaugh had made the decision to hold Lewis out until he was really ready to play. Lewis was admittedly rusty in his first game, but he made adjustments and eventually felt comfortable. "Me being the competitor, I worked so hard in the offseason, I strained it here in camp," Lewis said. "I didn't have any days off in the offseason. I was going so hard. That strain definitely sat me down a little bit. Take time off and let your body heal and rest. You could say it was a plus I got some time off. I wouldn't have taken that time off myself. "

In his return Lewis was part of one of the more memorable moments of the Michigan-Penn State game. After the game he was trying to live down the ultimate humiliation for a kick returner. He was tackled by enormous 5'10", 258-pound Penn State kicker Joey Julius on a kickoff, which Lewis returned 18 yards to the Michigan 24-yard line. He said he had never been caught by a kicker. "I did not see him at all," Lewis said, smiling. "He definitely thought he was going to make the tackle and he did."

He then jokingly threw Peppers under the bus. "I'll put this out there: I'm not trying to throw shade, but Jabrill did miss him," Lewis said, adding he gave Peppers an earful for missing the block when he had the chance. Lewis went with the pro move to acknowledge the embarrassment of the tackle before his teammates gave him a hard time. But they still did. "Everybody else definitely was laughing at me," Lewis said. "That's a cardinal sin—don't get caught by the kicker."

A few days later, Lewis joked that he had seen replays of his annihilation at the hands of Julius "a lot." Players from around the country, like LSU's Leonard Fournette and Iowa's Desmond King, an old friend of Lewis' from Detroit, contacted him to poke fun for getting tackled by a kicker. "That moment wasn't the best," Lewis said.

Harbaugh was not surprised by what transpired. He and his staff were well-acquainted with Julius' ability. "We know him well," Harbaugh said. "We've been watching him on tape, played against him last year. He is quite aggressive. He's a real football player playing kicker, and you don't find that very often. He's definitely the exception. He's like a heat-seeking missile out there, and we didn't get him blocked, and he had a free shot on Jourdan Lewis. He weighs 267, 270 pounds, and Jourdan took a shot but was able to get right back up and keep going. That's a natural smelling salt in the game of football. You get to get popped."

Lewis reached out and contacted Julius. "He told me it was luck really," Lewis said. "He don't like to tackle so he told me it was luck. So I got hit by luck." The two exchanged a few messages, and Lewis said he was gratified to know Julius also felt the impact of that hit. Although that hit might have hurt his pride a bit, Lewis admits that it hurt his body as well. "It really hurt, I have to be honest," he said. "I haven't been through anything like that physically in a while, had to get used to it, get in the training room, and get my body right."

But at 4–0 on the season, everyone was feeling good and feeling right. Lewis, among others on the team, also was feeling good about exercising the right to silently protest during the national anthem. Sparked by San Francisco 49ers quarterback Colin Kaepernick, who Harbaugh had coached while with the 49ers, demonstrations among college athletes had picked up steam after fatal police shootings of black men earlier in the week. After he refused to stand for the anthem during an exhibition game, Kaepernick's protest created controversy. It was an action he would continue to make throughout the season.

Before the Penn State game, a number of Michigan players, including Lewis, opted to raise their right fist during the anthem. Lewis said he meant no disrespect to the country but felt a message needed to be sent. Lewis, who had become vocal via social media on societal issues, said he wanted the public to know there is injustice in the country. "I have a platform," Lewis said. "Regardless of anything I'm going to stand up for injustice. This wasn't disrespecting anything. I love this university. I love this country, but things can get better. There's injustice here in this country, and we have to take notice of it. That's really what it is. It's nothing [of] disrespect toward the country or anything like that, but it is injustice. We've got to come together. Honestly, we have to encounter each other more. We have to be involved with each other more. We can't just think, *Okay, well, it is injustice, how do we fix it from the outside?* We have to come together as a human race."

Harbaugh wants his players to be informed and he wants them to feel free to express themselves. When asked about Kaepernick, he had said that he understood his motivation and right to protest but did not agree with the method he chose to express himself. Lewis, who had been raising his fist the first three weeks while he was injured and on the sideline, said a small group of players had discussed during Penn State week doing something along those lines. They did not want to force anyone to join.

Harbaugh, who had not yet spoken to his players about how to handle social protest or how to use the stage they have as college athletes, did not know before the game that the players planned to raise their fists. He took a stand in a sense after the game, a stand for his players.

"I've been thinking a lot about this over the last four, five, six weeks," Harbaugh said after the win. "Because I am the football coach doesn't mean I can dictate to people what they believe. I support our guys. I think this is something—it's not going away. It's gonna keep happening. I think we're a team as a country. I'll tell you what I believe in. I believe in God. I believe in country. I believe in family. I believe in rules of law and following rules. I believe as a team the things that we embrace, we should embrace. If something is not good for somebody on the team, then we talk about it, and we get it fixed together, as a team. Those are the things that I believe. But that doesn't mean that just because I'm a football coach that I can tell other people what to believe or what to think. I support people speaking their own mind and saying what they believe."

11

A Top Ten Test

When Jim Harbaugh arrived he decided to change the road uniforms to replicate the all-white versions he remembered the Wolverines wearing in 1974 when he was a kid hanging around the team and his dad was an assistant coach. He also brought back a time-honored tradition started under Bo Schembechler—helmet stickers. Schembechler's teams from 1969 to 1982 were awarded helmet stickers, and then after a brief hiatus, he brought them back from 1985 to 1989. Gary Moeller, who succeeded Schembechler, still had helmet stickers through 1994, but Lloyd Carr opted to keep the winged helmet clean from 1995 until Harbaugh took over.

Remember, Harbaugh likes to earn trophies and awards—academic, athletic, anything—and this is another award for which the players would strive. There are different criteria—one sticker for a victory, two stickers for a Big Ten win. There's a sticker for team turnover margin, unit stickers for defense, and other offense and individual awards earn them as well. "It's another way to create an environment of competition," tight end Jake Butt said. "They're pretty sweet."

As fourth-ranked and 4–0 Michigan prepared for Wisconsin in the final game of a five-game home stretch to open the season, Harbaugh brought up the helmet stickers as a way to demonstrate just how good Jabrill Peppers had been through the first third of the season. Through those games he had more stickers than anyone on the team and was absolutely flooring Harbaugh with his ability. Harbaugh typically dishes out praise, but with Peppers, even beginning as far back as the Chicago Big Ten Media Days, he had taken it to a new level. "He's good at football," Harbaugh liked to say, always drawing a laugh with that line because of its over-simplicity. He even laughed. "He's got just under 40 [stickers]. Four weeks in a row, he's No. 1 ranked."

Even Wisconsin coach Paul Chryst on Monday piled on the Peppers admiration. "He's a special football player," Chryst said. "There's two things when I think of him. One is there aren't a lot of players that can impact the game in all three phases like he does. And then when you watch him some more, he does a lot of the little things that are kind of reserved for when you specialize. That's what's impressive—his knowledge and awareness of the game. Clearly, as an athlete, he's special. But I think the football part of him, the understanding, that's what to me really makes him. He's gotta be the best player in college football right now."

Harbaugh loved coaching quarterback Andrew Luck because of his football IQ and his ability to grasp a new play almost instantly. In Peppers he had something very similar. Here was a primarily defensive player, who was also exceptional on special teams, running a play after a brief appearance in an offensive meeting. "It's that quick," Harbaugh said. "Quick nod and then he does it flawlessly. It's the darndest thing I've ever seen. Everybody really marvels at what he knows, what he has to know in a game, and the way he executes it."

Peppers ran his new offensive assignment with ease and changed the way it had been run in the 10 years Harbaugh has used it. "He was a running back and he was blocking," Harbaugh said. "His assignment was to block. He blocked and then he went out for a route. He got his blocking assignment done and then he continued out into a route. We threw it to him, which was not the design, but from now on, going forward and, we've been running this play for 10 years, we've never had a back that got his blocking assignment done and got into the route at the same time. He did it the first time as natural, like that was the way the play should have been run for the last 10 years. That's the kind of stuff he does. It breaks the mold darn near every time he does something. It's the darndest thing I've ever seen."

Harbaugh said Peppers by this point had made it perfectly clear he wanted to play as much as possible. This was a change from the previous season. Harbaugh described scenes from 2015 where he would be looking for Peppers on a tightly packed sideline and would yell: "Hey, get me Jabrill! Where's Jabrill?"

Fast forward a season, and Harbaugh no longer had to look far. "I would just say, 'Jabrill!' And he'd be, 'Yeah, I'm here, Coach! Right here!' Two feet behind me," Harbaugh said. "He's like a bull pawing at the ground ready to attack. It's good. Sometimes I didn't even get 'Jab...' and he said, 'I'm here, Coach. Right here.' It's exciting.

"He's good at football."

Very good. And everyone noticed. "It's daily with the team: 'Look what he did there. Look at what he did today,'" Harbaugh said. "He does it with a real genuine enthusiasm. Those eye-popping plays happen every day [in practice]. You give him something new, whether it's an offensive snap, know he hasn't done it before, and he goes out to practice, and everybody's looking. Nobody's done it that well. Guys who play that position don't do it that well. He's really good at football; that's kind of become what we say."

Michigan was brimming with confidence after improving to 4–0, but the Wolverines under Harbaugh lacked a signature win. Sure, the bowl game against Florida on New Year's Day was impressive, but they needed a win to turn heads. The Wolverines were 0–11 against top 10 opponents—mostly Ohio State—since 2008, heading into the game against No. 8 Wisconsin. The Badgers already had two top 10 victories this season. They beat then-No. 5 LSU in the opener and upset then-No. 8 Michigan State the previous week in East Lansing, Michigan, the first time since 1962 the Badgers had defeated two top 10 teams in a season. They, too, were feeling confident and likely would provide Michigan its biggest test of the season.

Wisconsin was ranked No. 1 in the Big Ten in rush defense and No. 1 in scoring defense. "Big team," Harbaugh said. "I'm wondering if the field's gonna be wide enough. They play extremely hard. High, high energy, tough, guys that can run and a big, physical team."

It would be a reunion of sorts for Harbaugh and Chryst, considering their families go way back. Their fathers, George Chryst and Jack Harbaugh, were football coaches, and their kids got to know each other. "It's been a family friendship, the Chrysts and the Harbaughs, going all the way back to 1987," Harbaugh said. "Our dads were friends; the sons were friends. It's been a 30-year friendship."

Harbaugh has always appreciated the history of his father's coaching relationships and values that they continue to the next generation in some cases, just as this one. Paul Chryst was a favorite of his. "If someone can't get along with Paul Chryst, there's probably something wrong with them," Harbaugh said. "That's the way I've always looked at it. He's a great guy to get along with. A great guy's guy. A great family guy. In all regards it's time well spent being around Paul Chryst."

Harbaugh was a quarterback for the San Diego Chargers in 1999 and 2000 while Paul Chryst was coaching tight ends under Mike Riley, now the Nebraska head coach. Geep Chryst, Paul's brother, was the offensive coordinator for the Chargers at that time, as well. When Harbaugh became head coach of the San Francisco 49ers in 2011, he hired Geep Chryst as offensive coordinator, so the family connection is deep.

Harbaugh joked about how many hours the Badgers work because of their sizable lines and how well they were playing. "I'd like to see an investigation into the Wisconsin team to see if they're complying with the 20-hour rule," he said. "They are really good. They are well-coached. It almost looks like they're spending a lot of time at it. A tip of the cap there. They've got a heck of a football team. They've done a great job over there. They're going to be darn tough to beat. We understand that. If we play at our best, we'll be darn tough to beat, too. It will be a real good football team."

The Badgers would prove tough to beat, but the Wolverines, with so many goals in place, needed the win over a top 10 opponent obviously to stay unbeaten—but also to prove that they had the ability to compete with the big boys.

Michigan missed three field goals in the game against the Badgers and struggled to take advantage of strong field position and more importantly lost starting left tackle Grant Newsome to a gruesome knee injury. But the defense had an impressive showing, including a highlight-worthy one-handed interception by Jourdan Lewis at the end of the game to seal the 14–7 victory.

Channing Stribling had two interceptions in the game, but Lewis' phenomenal one-hander on fourth down near the Wisconsin 46-yard line with just more than two minutes left was stunning. Lewis said he jumped a bit early and because of that couldn't use both hands to defend the throw intended for George Rushing. "The ball was in the air, and I knew I had to make a play on it—either knock it down or do what I did," Lewis said. "I jumped too early so I couldn't go get it with two. So I put my hand up there and see what happens. It was a great play. I'm just glad I could seal the deal for my team. It was definitely crazy. It was instincts [taking] over. I wasn't thinking at the moment."

It was the talk of the postgame and became a highlight video staple that week. "When I saw the ball go up, I was like, 'All right. We should be all right,'" running back Ty Isaac said. "Then I saw him jump and I wasn't sure if he jumped too early or not, but it just seemed like he hung up there forever. When he came down with the ball, everybody kind of looked around and was like, 'Did we just see that? Did that just happen?' It was crazy. He's a great athlete, and that was a great play."

Quarterback Wilton Speight was mesmerized. "I see him make a lot of plays, but that was on another level." Speight said. "He jumped and floated for five yards, and somehow caught it with one hand. That's a guy who's going to be playing on Sundays for a long time, glad he's on our team."

And Harbaugh was thoroughly impressed. "I've seen Odell Beckham Jr. do that," Harbaugh said, "looked like that kind of play. The most impressive thing about it, he jumped a little early. And I was a little nervous he was going to come down, and the ball was just going to go over his fingertips. But he was able to hang in the air and made a spectacular play. Then I was thinking, *It's fourth down. It probably would have been better had he not intercepted it.* I'm really glad he did because it was a spectacular, spectacular football play, an athletic play, really unbelievable."

Beyond Lewis' stunning interception, it was an important victory for Harbaugh and the Wolverines to establish themselves. They had been criticized for having played five straight games at home to open the season and not having the challenge of going on the road that deep into the season. After outscoring their first four opponents 208–55, upending talented Wisconsin was a badge of honor for the Wolverines. "We talked about it all week: it's probably going to be a close game, it's probably going to be physical, it's probably going to come down to the end," Isaac said. "We didn't put as many points on the board as we wanted to, but this was a game we expected to be a 14–7 game, something like that. Any time you can beat a top 10 team and let the world know we've got something going on here, we've got a great defense, and it's special."

What exactly was so special? What exactly was going on? What did Harbaugh have them believing? Were they paying attention to the rankings he had told them to embrace? What was going on with this program that they were starting to feel comfortable enough with their swagger? "It's not like fluke stuff," Isaac said. "We're playing physical. We have really a good defense, the offense is playing well. We respect everybody's game in this conference, but we have that confidence in knowing each man next to you is going to play as hard as they can for as long as they can."

The Wolverines had drawn a different level of confidence from beating Wisconsin in a slug-out game. "It says a lot about our team," receiver Amara Darboh said. "Wisconsin is a very tough football team, a very good defense, a very good offense. Us beating this team says a lot about our character and says a lot about our players. [But] this win doesn't define our season."

The other takeaway from the Wisconsin game was more evidence of how willing Harbaugh is to try new wrinkles on offense—in part to give his players a bit of a fun diversion and also develop another way to confound a defense. On the final play of the first quarter, Michigan had some fun and trotted out an "I formation." Like, a *real* I formation—10 players lined up in a line with Speight to the side. They then broke the chain and lined up normally. In its debut the quirky formation led to a five-yard gain by De'Veon Smith to the Badgers' 1-yard line.

Harbaugh said his son, Jay, the tight ends coach, had come up with the play called "Train." "Guys had fun with it," Jim Harbaugh said. "Put it in this week and executed it well."

At its initial reveal in an offensive meeting the previous week, the players were perplexed. "When they handed us—you know we get our playbooks—we get the sheets, and I'm looking at it and kind of looked back at [running backs] Coach Wheatley like, 'Is this play supposed to be horizontal, or is it supposed to be like this?'" Isaac said. "He was like, 'Wait, you'll see.' It works. It confuses people. They're creative and they know what they're doing. It's just putting [defensive players] out of their position and see if you can catch them off guard."

Speight said he knew the offense was in for something when the staff came into the meeting room with the play. Jay Harbaugh, "head man" Harbaugh, as Speight calls him, Tim Drevno, and Jedd Fisch were smirking when they walked in. "We knew something was going in that they liked, and it happened to be that play," Speight said. "The bottom line is if you do something like that you'd better not mess it up. You'd better pick up the first down, and we were able to do that. I'm sure it's pretty confusing for the defense. You see 10 dudes in a line. That probably would throw you off a little bit."

After the fact the players shook their heads in that what-is-Harbaugh-going-to-come-up-with-next manner. "When we heard that play was going in, we were like, 'Just another thing Harbaugh does,'" receiver Jehu Chesson said. "We followed it with blind faith. We were really excited we had that in this week. It was fun to rep it in practice, that's for sure."

Having faced the Train in practice, Lewis said it easily confuses a defense because they don't know what personnel an offense is getting in. Harbaugh encourages his staff to come up with original plays. Of course "original" in college football coaching terms usually means borrowing and adding your own twist or style.

Jay Harbaugh found the play while watching tape of a tight end prospect. "I can't take credit for that one," Jim Harbaugh said. "That was Jay Harbaugh. He was pouring over high school tape and saw a high school team in Colorado that used that. We can't take credit for it. If any credit I give it to Jay for spotting it, being diligent going through the tape. We said, 'That looks good.'"

According to the sleuthing of a Colorado High School writer, the school that used the Train was Chatfield High School in Littleton. Jay Harbaugh had just offered a recruit from Chatfield, which explains why he was watching the film. Chatfield coach Bret McGatlin told CHSSA.com he calls the play "Speed Line." It was created by his father, Don, and is part of their "Psycho" offense. "Our goal is to line up in less than three seconds," he said. "You really catch teams off guard. It really is crazy."

The Wolverines would use the play throughout the season. "We had fun practicing it," Jim Harbaugh said. "We had fun putting it in and putting it in the game. It might have a future."

At 5–0 and their ranking settled in at No. 4, the Wolverines still hadn't ventured out of Ann Arbor. It is important for teams to be road tested, particularly early. Usually one non-conference game is played away from Michigan Stadium, but the schedule had been set for several years, and that was the hand Michigan had been dealt.

In terms of building confidence in a first-year quarterback, having five games at home to start the season certainly was ideal for Speight. But as a competitor, he wanted to get that test.

The Wolverines finally were set to head outside of Michigan for the first time—and to New Jersey to face Rutgers in a night game. Michigan had lost there two years earlier, giving the Scarlet Knights their first Big Ten victory since joining the league. "It's October, and we haven't been on the road yet, but we're excited to get out of Ann Arbor and take an opponent on in their house," Speight said. "Two years ago we went to Rutgers, it was a hectic crowd, and they stormed the field. We just need to keep our composure and play football. There's no ifs, ands, or buts about it. Just play the game."

12

Jersey Boys

A FEW MONTHS BEFORE JIM HARBAUGH WAS HIRED AT Michigan, the Wolverines suffered one of the many lows of that season at Rutgers, falling 26–24 at High Point Solutions Stadium. It was so monumental a victory in a night-game setting for the Big Ten newcomers that the Scarlet Knights fans stormed the field and tore down the goal posts to celebrate. It was, for lack of a better word, embarrassing for the Wolverines.

While Michigan had walloped Rutgers at Michigan Stadium in Harbaugh's first season, the players, who were on that 2014 team and remembered the pain of being on that field and seeing the swarm of fans, were not keen to talk about it.

This was a different team. The Wolverines were now 5–0 and still ranked No. 4 and they were preparing for their first road game of the season. Memories of that game had been buried. Sort of. "I don't remember much about that game," offensive lineman Kyle Kalis said. What about the Rutgers fans storming the field? "That did happen. I do remember that," he said. "That's not going to happen again." Jake Butt remembered watching those Rutgers fans. "Yeah," he said. "Vaguely. Yeah."

While the veterans chose to avoid, for the most part, discussion of the last trip to Rutgers, there was a growing threat that Hurricane Matthew might threaten the East Coast, including New Jersey. During the 2015 season, Michigan's game at Maryland was moved from a primetime kickoff to noon because of a hurricane threat. "We're preparing to play the game when they tell us to play it," Harbaugh said.

This week was personal for many of the players because of the large presence of New Jersey-natives, like Jabrill Peppers and

Rashan Gary, not to mention linebackers coach Chris Partridge, who had been coach at Paramus Catholic in New Jersey, where those two had played high school football.

Although Chris Ash, the first-year coach at Rutgers, coined "Fence the Garden" as a program motto to encourage the top talent to stay home, many of the top players were already long gone to programs like Michigan. Harbaugh and his staff maintained a presence in New Jersey over the summer by holding a satellite camp at Paramus Catholic, and Ash, the former defensive coordinator at Ohio State, was joined by Ohio State coach Urban Meyer and held a rival camp.

During the Big Ten Media Days in Chicago, Ash was asked if he was ready to embrace what was called a "fan rivalry" between Michigan and Rutgers. Ash said there was no rivalry with Michigan. Yet. "They've done some things that we have not been able to do," Ash said. "I think it's great for fans to get a chance in the offseason to talk about college football. I have a tremendous amount of respect for Coach Harbaugh and the job that he's done at Michigan and the program that they've had for a number of years. We're doing the best we can at Rutgers to create rivalries with everybody that we play. It's great that the fans are involved, care, and are passionate about what we're doing at Rutgers."

Still, Ash had felt compelled to create the "Fence the Garden" motto, in part because of Harbaugh's presence in New Jersey recruiting. Michigan had targeted Northern Jersey, which features what Michigan defensive backs coach Mike Zordich described as a "better brand of high school football" than exists in the rest of the state. He had played for the Philadelphia Eagles and was already familiar with the talent level in neighboring New Jersey.

With nine players from New Jersey on the roster, this was a big, big week. The Jersey Boys were going home, they would play before family and friends in a night-game setting. And they needed tickets. "A lot of tickets being asked for from everyone," senior Matt Godin said, laughing.

Kalis said the demand for tickets from the Jersey players has been so great, he resorted to rock, paper, scissors to determine who would get his. The winner? Rashan Gary.

Peppers, Michigan's most well-known player and a triple-threat; Gary; and Juwann Bushell-Beatty, who would start at left tackle in place of injured Grant Newsome, also played at Paramus Catholic for Partridge. They are proud of being from New Jersey, they are proud they sound a little different than everyone else with their East Coast accents, and they want everyone to know the Garden State has plenty of really fine players. "[There are] a lot of talented guys in New Jersey," Bushell-Beatty said. "I can say from firsthand experience I've played against a lot of talent there. There are a lot of guys who come out of there who are go-getters who are ready to go."

Interestingly, Zordich said that often the best football talent finds its ways into pockets of certain states. Northeastern Ohio, for instance, has always been a strong base of high school football—just as Northern Jersey had become. The North Jersey players have a swagger and are, from all accounts, tough, tough guys. "Maybe just certain areas are tougher than others," Zordich said. "The proof's in the pudding. I'm not from Jersey, so I can't compare anything. I just know where I lived in South Jersey [while with the Eagles] is a little different than some parts of North Jersey. It's just what I see."

And Harbaugh knew where to find these tough players. And what the Jersey players found is once a few of them went to Michigan, it made it easier to follow suit because they liked the idea of being with former teammates and also guys they played against. Harbaugh had gone to New Jersey the last two summers to hold satellite camps, and as the team prepared to face Rutgers, the NCAA proposed to limit the number of days programs can hold summer camps and clinics. Harbaugh opted to take a positive approach to the decision that he clearly had provoked.

The NCAA Division I Council has proposed a change to football camps and clinics to improve the recruiting environment, effectively limiting the summer satellite camp tour of which Harbaugh had been a strong advocate and participant. Harbaugh and his staff had launched that ambitious national—in addition to stops in Samoa and Australia—schedule of satellite camps during the previous summer, and under pressure from the SEC and ACC conferences, the NCAA proposed that programs could have no more than 10 days for holding or participating in football camps and clinics. They do not have to be 10 days in succession, but that was a reduction from two, 15-day periods.

Harbaugh was upbeat when asked about the proposed changes during the week on his Detroit radio appearance. "That would take away a lot of fun. We did close to 50 last year, and that was a lot of fun," Harbaugh said. "Heck, if every school was doing 10, that would probably be more than what was done last year, so possibly it's a really good thing. Everybody carries the water, but the main thing is football is being spread around the country, and youngsters are getting good coaching, and they have opportunities to show what they can do. Potentially, it's got a chance to be really good, so I can't say that's a negative. The only negative is we'll have less fun."

When it was suggested to Harbaugh that the NCAA was outright targeting him with this rule, he seemed to play coy. "It's a Michigan rule?" Harbaugh asked.

"It's a Jim Harbaugh rule," the show hosts responded.

Harbaugh, as is his way in situations like this, opted not to react. He had to know the rule was directed at him, but he chose not to acknowledge it in that way and decided to be unwavering in his positive approach to the proposal. What he saw was another jab at the game that he has sought to protect and promote, something his brother, John, and father, Jack, have joined him in advancing. "If you look at it and did the math, if everybody did 10, that would be phenomenal, that would be a lot, that would be phenomenal for the youngsters who are being introduced to football or reintroduced to football at the high school level," Harbaugh said. "Guys that want to get better, they really like football. That's what we found last year when we went around the country was that football's really strong in America. Youngsters really like football. They want to play it. It does a lot for them physically, mentally. It teaches them how to do so many things, including competing and going out and doing your best, but you need coaching. You need time on task with football. You get better at football by playing football. More is more, not less is more. I'm going to be for it, that it could be a real positive. Look at the bright side. Less fun for us, but more coaching for all the guys out there who want to play football."

A day before the team departed for New Jersey, the hurricane was no longer an issue as it had spun away offshore and not moved north. It did rain before and during the game, but that did not put a damper on anything. The Scarlet Knights were a big underdog, and the Wolverines proved why.

They dismantled the Scarlet Knights 78–0. Including their loss to Ohio State a week earlier, Rutgers was outscored 136–0 in its last two games. It was Michigan's third largest margin of victory in program history, and the Wolverines improved to 6–0 heading into a bye week.

Michigan was dominating in every aspect. There were nine rushing touchdowns, including one from a backup, backup fullback, Bobby Henderson, who grew up nearby in New York and was able to enjoy that special moment with his parents and old friends in the stadium. Wilton Speight sat after the first half, giving backup quarterbacks John O'Korn and Shane Morris a chance to play, and the defense was stifling.

While the offense churned 605 yards of offense, the defense held the Scarlet Knights to 39 yards, including five yards passing. They had two first downs that did not come until late in the game when Michigan's backups were in. Rutgers was 0-for-17 on third down. That kind of production didn't make the Michigan defensive players satisfied. It made them hungry, feeding off Harbaugh's rhythm of being better tomorrow and the next day.

They had believed all along they were the best defense in the country. "At this point we try to improve even more," UM defensive lineman Taco Charlton. "We set the bar and we keep trying to improve. We go out there and try to be the best defense in the country. It can't just stop with Rutgers. We have to improve this bye week and once we go on to Illinois we keep on improving and show the country what we're really made of. The goal was to be the best D-line in the country, and we knew we had to prove that, and where that starts is being able to rush four, and that's what Coach Mattison preaches to us since I've been here, to be able to rush four. I feel like the last couple of weeks we've been able to do that."

"There is no backups. That's what we preach on the defense," Peppers said. "Every time you go out there, you're expected to play like a starter. We don't look at the scoreboard. We want to impose our will as fast and as hard as we can. The younger guys are starting to adapt to that because it's up to us to set the foundation. I definitely think they're starting to buy in and trusting the coaches and trust what the older guys are telling them."

For Peppers it was an absolutely fitting homecoming. He was injured and could not play in 2014 when the Wolverines were at Rutgers, but he did accompany the team and was spirited on the sideline as he tried to motivate. "I definitely wanted to come out and make a statement with the guys tonight," Peppers said, "couldn't ask for a better victory. I've never been part of a victory this massive. You've got to handle it with class and keep improving next week. You can't stay on your high horse."

Harbaugh, though, got on that high horse for Peppers and made it absolutely clear how good he is in case no one had noticed. Peppers scored two touchdowns, taking direct snaps out of a wildcat formation, and had a punt return for a touchdown called back. Through six games Peppers had 442 all-purpose yards and a punt return touchdown in addition to his work on defense.

In the postgame news conference, Harbaugh campaigned for Peppers as a Heisman Trophy candidate. This was quite a departure for Michigan, which had never promoted a player for a major national award. But there was Harbaugh, putting it all out there, knowing, of course, he would have plenty of New York media taking down every word. "Gosh, if there's a better player in the country, I don't know who it is," Harbaugh said. "I know there's a lot of great players out there, but to be able to coach a guy like Jabrill Peppers is a real joy. There's just so much more. He can throw. There's nothing he can't do. It's the darndest thing I've ever seen. My humble opinion, I believe that [you're looking] at a Heisman Trophy winner."

Harbaugh was asked if he has coached someone as versatile as Peppers. "No, not even close," Harbaugh said. "A lot of great players and I hate to compare because somebody gets diminished. If there's a bible sitting right here, I'd put my hand on it and say, 'No, I have not coached a more versatile player than Jabrill Peppers.'"

Harbaugh eventually came up with what he believed was an appropriate comparison—the legendary Jim Thorpe. Peppers said he had a little bit of extra motivation playing in New Jersey. He said it was the first time since high school that many of his friends and family got a chance to see him play. "Whenever you get a chance to get the ball in your hands, you want to make something positive," said Peppers, who also made what appeared to be a spectacular punt return for a touchdown that was called back because of a penalty. "God had his hand on me today. Some of those plays, I can't really describe it. I have to give it all to the blocking, the coaching scheme. They set the guys up in positions to excel."

Speight was dumbfounded watching Peppers play at Rutgers, particularly on his 63-yard gain. "That play where the running back went the wrong way, and he turned and he wasn't there, so he took off, as he was running, I was like, this kid looks like a guy I created in NCAA football on my Xbox," Speight said. "To have a guy not only this good at football and you hear him talking right now, it's not just for the cameras. It's behind closed doors. He's a great teammate."

The Wolverines jumped on the Peppers For Heisman bandwagon. "He's the best player in all of college football," right tackle Erik Magnuson said. "The versatility alone is just unbelievable. The impressive part is he really doesn't practice that much with the offense, but you give him the ball in the game, and he makes plays. He's the best player I've ever seen in my life. He's so fast and so explosive he can turn a little hole into a 50-yard gain."

"Jabrill is something that's rare. You've never seen it before," fullback Khalid Hill said. "The stuff he does, he can literally come to the offensive side and produce the way that he does and go to defense and do the same thing and do it at a high level is amazing. He's also in on all returns. It's crazy."

Not only incredibly versatile, Peppers on the defensive side also entered the game fifth nationally in tackles for loss with a 1.9 average. "The Heisman Trophy is for the best player in college football," Harbaugh said. "He's the best player in college football."

He also is a young man who has endured enormous personal challenges. During the 2015 season, he wrote a moving first-person piece in The Player's Tribune about the pain of not having his father, Terry Peppers, as he grew up. Terry Peppers was sent to prison on firearms charges when Peppers was seven years old. Since his father is now out of prison, the two are gradually reconnecting.

In 2010 Peppers' older half-brother, Don Curtis, was shot and killed near their home in East Orange, New Jersey. His brother, who had always been his biggest promoter, was gone. "He was the one who called it, actually," Peppers said. "I can hear him now saying, 'I told you, little bro, stick to the plan.' I was probably eight or nine, it was probably my third year playing. He was like, 'Little bro, if anybody can make it, it is you.' When he told me that, I was like, 'Yeah, right.' I was the youngest out of my cousins and my brothers. Typically, the youngest gets picked on the most, and you've got to play with old guys. I finally got a chance to play with people my age, and it was just easy. It felt natural. A lot of things he instilled in me, I still carry."

Charles Woodson was one voice Peppers had listened to for guidance and advice, and he also had become friendly with Reggie Bush. Peppers wore No. 5 as a tribute to Bush, someone he said he emulated growing up playing football. Peppers was more, though, than the most versatile player in the game. His is an effervescent personality who matches the energy he takes to the football field. He is flashy and exuberant, but he's also humble, as he was after the Rutgers game, reminding everyone to not get on a high horse even after an enormous victory. "I don't like the attention at all, actually," he said. "It's a double-edged sword. I just want to play football so my mom doesn't have to pay for college, help better my family. People are constantly at me on Twitter, saying stuff they would never say if they were in my presence. It's just crazy to me. Like my brother always told me, 'To whom much is given, much is expected.' So it's my responsibility to handle it the right way."

13

Kicking the Shins

THE STATE OF MICHIGAN HAS A POPULAR "PURE Michigan" ad campaign that highlights so many of the wonderful aspects of the state like the lakes, the golf courses, the winter sports. A soothing voice and pleasant music guide you through the commercials that ultimately make viewers at least consider visiting and exploring the state.

It would not be surprising to hear Jim Harbaugh's voice one day in those commercials describing the benefits of global warming. That's right—global warming. Two days after the big win at Rutgers and with a weekend off before playing Illinois, Harbaugh was in a great mood on his radio show and seemed to be a one-man "Pure Michigan" show as he talked about the wonderful seasons.

On that October day, it had been 80 degrees, and Harbaugh was feeling tremendously upbeat about the pure Michigan weather. "Now we're the new Mediterranean—a lot of coastline, and how about that out there today? Eighty degrees out there," Harbaugh said brightly. "It is so beautiful here. It's awesome. Global warming is good for Michigan. It's good for recruiting."

He was appalled by show host Jim Brandstatter, who chimed in that everything in Michigan is great until February and the snow and the cold it brings. "Why do people always say that?" Harbaugh said. "The one complaint I have about Michigan people—it can be a beautiful fall day like it was today or a beautiful summer day or a beautiful spring day, and it's 'Wait till winter comes.' I happen to like the changing of the seasons. I like the feeling of snow crunching under my feet. It doesn't get any better. There's no better place to be in the fall, spring, summer. The winters are beautiful. We've got it all here. It's the changing of the seasons. I don't know how you could have it any better."

If he was practicing a recruiting pitch to a potential recruit in the South or the West, it went well judging by the approval from the crowd. He also went on to praise engineers. Apparently, when Michigan doesn't have a game to prepare for in a particular week, Harbaugh takes the opportunity to discuss a number of things. He called Michigan's engineering school "magnificent." "Personally, I think it's the best degree you can get in college, an engineering degree, some form or fashion," he said, "just to be able to think like an engineer. Everything is engineering. Just the way they think, solving problems, one step to the next, it's a real blessing for someone to have the talent to be an engineer. And you know what? They never disappoint in football either. I've never had an engineering student who hasn't figured out how to be a good football player."

With Michigan off that Saturday, Harbaugh decided that after one day of practice, those who had played regularly would get the next three days off. That didn't mean they were really off, just not hitting. Instead, they would throw a whistle around their necks and coach the younger players. "Like a beaver dam, everybody doing something, everybody contributing and improving," Harbaugh said. "That's what we're looking for, to do the most we can. One-stone, two-birds idea. Players who haven't played as many plays or haven't played at all will be practicing a lot of fundamentals, a lot of technique, a lot of individual work. [The older players will] be able to physically get themselves back, and the ones who haven't been playing as much will get an opportunity to improve their game, which will help us next week and the rest of the season and next year."

Harbaugh is all about teaching moments and finding unique ways to stretch the experience of the players. Often those moments come after a player makes a mistake, on the field or off. But this was an opportunity to allow the veterans to lead in a different way while guiding the younger players and teaching them. It was also fun.

Senior nose tackle Ryan Glasgow quickly took to wearing a whistle, though he said he feared actually using it because defensive line coach Greg Mattison would have yelled at him. Although he thought of the whistle as more of a symbol, he relished the idea of coaching while resting his body. He enjoyed working with the young defensive lineman and sharing tips of his forte, which is technique. "It's nice to interact with them when they're not doing scout [team]," Glasgow said. "When they're the main focus of attention, you can kind of cater to them instead of when they're on the sidelines of games telling you what you're doing right, what you're doing wrong. It's nice to build a rapport with them and help them out instead of them helping you out all the time. Since I'm more of a technician on the field than anything, I like to help them out with technique and try to get their minds right for a practice. Coach Harbaugh's practices aren't easy, and when you're out there taking a lot of the reps, it can get tiring, and so we're trying to encourage them."

Harbaugh believes that having the more experienced players coach is a helpful exercise for them. "It's a good feeling to put the whistle on and coach a guy," Harbaugh said. "A lot of them do it already, but to do it full time during a practice, you learn a lot yourself. You learn a lot, crystalizes your thoughts when you have to tell somebody else what they could be doing better or give them a tip or a piece of advice."

For players who might consider coaching as a career after football, these few days with the whistle on gave them a taste of what they might expect. "It's fun to help the young guys and show them different things," defensive lineman Taco Charlton said. "It was a chance for us to step back and help them out and show them different things to help out their game for the future and help the success of Michigan football in the future."

Jake Butt, a team co-captain, was already used to coaching a bit. Since the summer he had worked with the young tight ends and considered himself, in a sense, an assistant coach to position coach

Jay Harbaugh. His role in the summer was more about leading by example, but he enjoyed taking on the bigger responsibility of coaching and being demanding during the three days. Center Mason Cole liked Harbaugh's two-birds, one-stone approach and said younger players react differently and positively when taking coaching from a peer. Cole found the experience good for the veterans as well as the youngsters.

The bottom line, though, was at the halfway point of the season and with the competition getting tougher, Harbaugh wanted to make sure the younger players received valuable reps so that going forward, if they were called on in a game, it wouldn't feel daunting. And if not for this season, he wanted to gauge their development as he looked ahead to not only the rest of the season, but also next season and beyond.

Harbaugh was in a great mood that Monday, following the rout of Rutgers, so it came as no surprise that the Wolverines, now ranked No. 4 with a 6–0 record and the nation's No. 1-ranked defense and an offense averaging 50 points a game—fourth best nationally, were feeling good about themselves. This is where they wanted to be, where they expected to be at the midpoint of the season. The break could not have been timed better, as the Wolverines would face a tougher second half of the season with three of their final six regular-season games on the road against in-state rival Michigan State, Iowa in a night game, and rival Ohio State. Nothing had surprised the Wolverines to this point. Expectations were high entering the season because they set them high and they were starting to feel even higher. Still, the players, who were definitely carrying themselves with a swagger and a confidence that hadn't been seen in the football building in quite some time, carefully held their emotions in check.

Did the players expect they would be this good? "You know what? I expected it, but sometimes you always have something in the back of your mind that maybe it might not go your way," Glasgow said. "But I'm really proud of how the team has prepared thus far in the season.

We still have another half to go, and I think with the preparation we've been putting in during game weeks and how hard we've been practicing I think we can finish with the Big Ten championships. I mean, why play the game if you don't think you can win a Big Ten championship? That's our goal. We're not very shy about it. We think we have the guys to do it, and we have the coaching staff to do it, and we've got the players."

Michigan had not won a Big Ten title since 2004, and Glasgow, like the rest of his senior teammates, understood better than most how a season can drift and become a disappointment. Butt, who way back in the spring had been the first to say the Wolverines had the talent to go all the way and challenge on the national scene, said the team had built confidence, even though the first half of the season was pockmarked by weaker opponents.

There, though, had been tests, and the Wolverines had survived unscathed. "Colorado, turns out they're a very good team, Wisconsin's a good team, Penn State's a pretty good team, too," Butt said. "We've had to respond to getting punched in the mouth and we've had our backs against the wall here and there, we've faced some adversity, and we've also handled the games that we were supposed to handle. We've got a little bit of everything. That being said, going into the season, we had a target on our back, and with each win and each week, that target has grown and we understand that. That's just going to continue to be the case going forward where everybody is going to want to knock us off and ruin our season. We understand that."

They also understood that they were enjoying success because they hadn't changed their attitude or approach. That's what Harbaugh had instilled—keep working hard, keep focusing, and maintain that each game is a championship game. "Thankfully, the mind-set we've had since last January is the mind-set we're going to carry through this whole entire season," Butt said. "We're not surprised to be here, we don't have to change who we are as a team, or who we are as leaders or players. We've adapted the mind-set: all we're going to do is work hard. We know we have great players, we know we have talent, we know we have the coaches. All we have to do is work and execute, and that's the mind-set we've had going forward. We're 6–0, we're not patting ourselves on the back. We're not too excited about that. You look at the past. We understand how quick a game can change and how quick a season can change, too, with a play here or a play there. Everything can be turned around real quick. We've learned from that and we're going to try to avoid that these upcoming weeks by working hard, by preparing, and continuing to execute."

Earlier that week while Harbaugh was on his radio show, he and Brandstatter laughed about a saying their coach, Bo Schembechler, had when he suspected his players were getting full of themselves. "As Bo would say, 'somebody tells you you're good, kick 'em in the shins,'" Harbaugh said.

Glasgow said that was exactly the current team's approach. No one would allow complacency to settle in, or else there would be a kick in the shins. "Everyone works as hard the next week as they did the last week," Glasgow said. "As Coach Harbaugh said, the longer it takes a team to figure out they're good, the better. I think there are a lot of people who don't know they're good yet and I think people work like they have something to prove every game and every week."

Clearly, Harbaugh had stressed—particularly during a bye week—that complacency is not a friend. "Our record speaks for that right now as we're undefeated," Butt said. "We're not patting ourselves on the back. This is where we wanted to be, this is where we were to be, this is where we really expected to be. We're just hungry for more at this point. What's better than being 6–0 is being 7–0 and then 8–0 and 9–0. We're going to continue to work toward those goals going forward."

With Michigan's continuing success, the Ruth's Chris Steak House in Ann Arbor was doing a booming business. Before the Rutgers game, the restaurant started a "Score Big" promotion, which offered patrons a percentage off the bill based on Michigan's margin of victory. Who knew Michigan would dismantle Rutgers 78–0? But Ruth's Chris then decided to cap the discount to 50 percent off the bill. When Harbaugh heard of the restaurant's discount deal, he said he was "tickled" by it. He also planned to take advantage of the deal. Despite the restaurant being sold out, restaurant general manager Buzz Goebel managed to squeeze in Harbaugh and his wife, Sarah, during the bye week. Harbaugh shared a photo via Twitter of them having dinner. Of course, his steak was accompanied by a glass of milk—that is his vitamin, after all. Steak and milk.

As the Wolverines got into game-week mode for Illinois, they had moved to No. 3 in the rankings. Although they had remained vigilant in their focus, they admitted to keeping tabs on rivals Michigan State and Ohio State. Michigan would face Michigan State a week after the Illinois game, and the Michigan players still could not quite get over the finish of the previous year's game, the fumbled punt with 10 seconds to go, and Michigan State taking it in for the victory with no time left. And then, there's always Ohio State looming at the end of the regular season.

Senior Kyle Kalis admitted to some peeking at Michigan State and Ohio State, particularly the previous week when the Wolverines did not have a game. It is only natural, of course, even with Illinois next on the schedule. "I want them to win all the way until we play them," Kalis, an Ohio native, said of Ohio State. "I know some of the guys were wishing them to lose. I mean, it's hard not to. A little part of me was hoping they'd lose. I'm glad they won. I want to make the game as meaningful as possible."

Kalis watched the Ohio State-Wisconsin game last Saturday. Harbaugh also said he watched that one and has been following Michigan State. "Definitely keep tabs on them a lot," Kalis said.

Michigan State was in the midst of a losing skid, and Kalis didn't hide his pleasure. "Makes me happy," Kalis said. "Makes me happy."

The Wolverines probably knew they had some room to allow their focus to drift from Illinois. Michigan trounced Illinois 41–8 on Homecoming to improve to 7–0 and 4–0 in the Big Ten. And with that victory, the Wolverines could turn their attention exclusively to Michigan State, which had won seven of the last eight in the rivalry. But it was the 2015 game that the Spartans won 27–23 after scoring on the fumbled punt that was the chief talking point for the players. "All I can say is really those last couple seconds are still boiling, like we still taste it in our mouths," running back De'Veon Smith, who scored a touchdown against the Illini, said. "We're going to give Michigan State all [we have] this week."

Smith and his teammates felt good about their performance against Illinois. It was balanced offensively with 291 passing yards and 270 rushing. And the defense held Illinois without a passing yard in the first half and 172 total yards for the game. "The execution was outstanding both offensively, defensively, special teams," Harbaugh said. "We just executed well, really, really impressed. The first three drives of the game and then the entire game, I thought Wilton Speight may have had one of his best games of his career. It was pretty windy out there. It was tough to throw. He was throwing the intermediate deep stuff, the 30-yard throws, the 35-yard, the 40-yard throws, just on the money. It was impressive. Sometimes it's never as good as you think until you look at the tape. I have a feeling that was the best he's played."

As Harbaugh spoke, he fidgeted a bit with his glasses. They were new. On the sideline he would frequently wear reading glasses, but after a recent visit to the eye doctor, he was told he needed to wear glasses all the time. "I'm now a full-time glasses person," he said. He made an interesting frame selection that carried much meaning for him. "This style in particular is a tip of the cap, a nod to Woody Hayes, to Michael Douglas in the movie *Falling Down*, and also a tip of the cap to Malcolm X," Harbaugh said. "In honor of those three men."

If Harbaugh was feeling a little sentimental because of his glasses, he also enjoyed having legendary baseball player Hank Aaron as the honorary captain. The 82-year-old Aaron, second on baseball's all-time home-run list with 755, visited with the Michigan baseball team for about a half hour before the football game. The visit was arranged by Aaron's granddaughter Emily Haydel, a Michigan undergrad who works with the Michigan football and baseball teams.

"He's such a great man, such a gentleman," Harbaugh said. "I was getting texts last night, some of the guys on the team were texting me how great Hank Aaron was. He talked to the team last night. You know when you're around greatness. He's one of the all-time greats, was really honored to share a sideline with Hank Aaron."

And now the focus officially turned to Michigan State.

14

The Paul Bunyan Trophy

J IM HARBAUGH ARRIVED IN ANN ARBOR TO TAKE OVER Michigan's football program at a time Michigan State, under coach Mark Dantonio, had become an enormously successful team not only in the annual rivalry game with the Wolverines, but also on the national scene. What each coach thinks of the other is always an important storyline. Harbaugh and Dantonio are entirely different in their approach, and in typical Michigan-Michigan State week form, Harbaugh was asked about his feelings regarding Dantonio. "He's done a great job," Harbaugh said, "one of the best college football coaching jobs in the history of the game, at the highest level."

Harbaugh, whose team had gone 12–1 since that crazy, final seconds loss to Michigan State the previous season, would not diminish the Spartans despite the fact they had dropped their last five games and were about to face the newly minted No. 2-ranked Wolverines. Michigan State, winless in the Big Ten, would host the Wolverines at Spartan Stadium, but the Spartans had won seven of the last eight meetings. "It doesn't matter what's happened before this week for us or for an opponent," Harbaugh said. "It never does. It matters what happens on the gameday. We know the task in front of us. We know the challenge. It's up to us to get prepared to play that game, so we go out there confident and execute and have a chance to be successful. They're a very good football team. We know we'll be tough to beat, and they'll be tough to beat."

Aside from preparing for Michigan State, Harbaugh, who wanted his players to embrace the rankings, also cautioned it was too early for his team to take what he called a "victory lap" despite ascending to the No. 2 national ranking with a defense ranked No. 1 in nearly every category. His players, who had been emphasizing that they couldn't settle, had completely bought into this approach. "It's not something that really even needs to be said," Jake Butt said. "We're not patting ourselves on the back. It goes back to: this is where we wanted to be and where we expected to be in all honesty, and I say that in a humble way just because of the way we worked this offseason, the way we prepared, we've got a great coaching staff, great leadership. Even the guys on the scout team are doing an unbelievable job of giving us great, great looks, week in and week out, allowing us to execute at such a high level on Saturday. There's a lot of football left to be played. We know it as well as anybody that anything can happen in this sport. We're not taking anything for granted."

Michigan's defense headed into the Michigan State game ranked No. 1 in five categories—total yards (207), scoring (10 points per game), passing yards (111 per game), first downs allowed (74), and third-down conversion (13 percent). The Wolverines also were second nationally in pass efficiency defense (84.19 rating), red-zone conversion (66.7 percent) and fourth in sacks (3.57 per game) and against the run (96 yards per game). "I say this all the time," quarterback Wilton Speight said. "It was probably the worst month of my life going against that defense every day during camp. I feel bad for quarterbacks every Saturday."

This would be the first Michigan-Michigan State game for Wolverines defensive coordinator Don Brown. Players over the years from both sides have called it the most physical and chippy game of the season. It has been referred to as a street fight and it is, of course, for state bragging rights and ownership for the year of thePaul Bunyan Trophy.

Brown noticed a difference immediately at the start of the practice week. "I can tell it's Michigan State week, I know that," Brown said. "Obviously, my first experience, so I'm kind of feeding off my guys. We're going to prepare exactly the same way we prepare each and every week. The reality is: if I tell you it's Michigan State week, and all of a sudden, we're going to buckle down in the staff room, then what have we been doing for seven weeks? It's the same for us in terms of the preparation. I get a sense from the guys it's a little bit more. There's no question about it. That would be a lie if I said it wasn't."

Brown wasn't at Michigan the year before. He didn't experience the disappointment the players felt when their victory became a loss in the final 10 seconds when Michigan punter Blake O'Neil fumbled the snap, and MSU's backup defensive back Jalen Watts-Jackson returned it for a touchdown and the 27–23 victory. "Whoa! He has trouble with the snap!" Sean McDonough, calling the game for ESPN, yelled, his voice cracking as he described the play.

"Obviously, it's a devastating play, it's a shock," senior Chris Wormley said. "You kind of scratch your head and say, 'What just happened?' But at the end of the day, we're a new team, this is a new season. You say, 'What can you do to get better?' And that's what we're doing this week."

Cornerback Jourdan Lewis called it a learning experience. "We corrected what happened on special teams and we moved forward," he said. "Coach Harbaugh always talked about we're going to handle this better than any other team could ever handle it. He was right. We've gone on and played the remainder of our games."

Taco Charlton agreed that this was a new Michigan team with seven wins under its belt. That play from the previous season was no longer relevant. But he did say the game was one the Wolverines had been waiting for. Dan Dierdorf worked the 2015 game as part of the Michigan radio broadcast and, while he hated its conclusion, he understood its value in terms of enhancing the college game. "In hindsight 10 things had to happen for Michigan State to score on that play, and it's so rare when all 10 of them happen," he said. "Of all players for that ball to go to, it goes to the guy who catches it perfectly in full stride heading to the end zone. It really was one of those plays that the cosmos aligned. You just don't see it where everything that Michigan State needed for that to happen, happened. It's so rare. It's a once-in-a-generation play. They don't come along like that very often. The fact it was against your arch rival, it was the old saying: 'We snatched defeat from the jaws of victory.' The big picture: plays like that are really good for college football. I'm sorry it happened, I'm devastated it happened, but if you take two steps back and look at the big picture, it's great for the game when something like that happens. Plays like that make people love college football. We took one for the team. I just wish it wouldn't have happened on my watch."

Harbaugh wasn't sure if he would show the team a video clip from the previous season because he was not clear what the value might be. "I've always thought that for guys in the arena, guys that are in the ring playing or on the field, that anytime you lose you have that feeling," Harbaugh said. "There's that feeling of loss, and it does not feel good. And every time you win, there's that great feel of winning, thrill of victory, wonderful feeling of winning. That's the nature of the competition."

During his weekly Detroit radio appearance, talk turned to recruiting. In explaining his decision to flip his commitment from Notre Dame to Michigan, defensive end recruit Donovan Jeter told his local paper one of the reasons why he pulled the trigger was Harbaugh. Jeter said Harbaugh "is the coolest dude I ever met in my life."

Harbaugh was asked about that on the show, though co-host Mike Stone was careful not to mention the recruit's name. Harbaugh answered in the most Harbaugh manner. "That's very flattering," Harbaugh said. "Usually, I don't make a great first impression, but I do grow on people after a while. Sometimes you hit it off right off the bat. I've made friends right off the bat here lately. It's been a good feeling. The best kind of love is when you love somebody, and they love you back. That's truly the best. And maybe the best is love at first sight when you really just hit it off right off the bat: you love somebody, and they love you back right away. Right at first sight, maybe that's the absolute best kind of love."

Harbaugh earlier in the week on his radio show spoke extensively about how Michigan's talent had developed into NFL talent and, though the NFL draft was months away, he felt confident that many would make the jump after the season. He has made the program accessible to NFL scouts and general managers. Harbaugh said he wants them to watch his players, and so Michigan rolls out the red carpet and has a room in Schembechler Hall designed just for their use to watch tape before and after they head to practice. Several scouts told Harbaugh how many good players he has. "I don't know how many guys we'll get drafted, but it'll be double digits," Harbaugh said on his radio show. "That's awesome."

He said opening the building to the scouts helps the players' cause. "Because you want to eyeball a guy," he said. "It's the same as a college coach when you go watch a high school game. You can see them in person. You can really see a 'dude' in person, as Don Brown would say, a guy that's a real player. We aspire for our guys to play at the very highest level, which is the NFL. So everything we can do to make it beneficial for our players to be seen, to be noticed, to be evaluated, the better."

Pro futures aside, by the time Saturday came along, the Wolverines, with a strong showing of Michigan fans at Spartan Stadium, wanted nothing more than to get the victory and get out of East Lansing with the Paul Bunyan Trophy. Michigan State trailed by as many as 20 points but never quit. The second-ranked Wolverines eventually prevailed 32–23 but not before some weaknesses in the defense were exposed. The Spartans, coming off a five-game losing streak, were big underdogs. And yet they hung around and hung around and tested the top-ranked Wolverines' defense.

Speight later said the defense bent a little more than usual and he was right. Michigan State was held to 148 yards in the first half, including 34 passing, but finished with 401. The Spartans had 253 second-half yards. "If you can't stay focused in the game, then that's a big red flag in any game," Jourdan Lewis said disgustedly after the game. "We can't do that. We got lucky, we definitely got lucky. We were definitely the more talented team, and that's how we won. We just stopped being focused. I have no idea what it was. We stopped concentrating like we did. The third quarter was probably our best quarter."

With a night game at Iowa and the regular-season finale at Ohio State ahead in the final month, Jabrill Peppers, who had a critical fourth-down stop late in the Michigan State game, said he welcomed this test from the Spartans. The 401 yards Michigan State gained were the most the Michigan defense had allowed all season. In back-to-back weeks in September, UCF gained 331 yards, and then Colorado had 325. Michigan State's 217 rushing yards were the second most Michigan had allowed this season behind UCF's 275 in the second week of the season. "We definitely needed that as a defense," Peppers said. "We definitely can't go into Iowa playing like that. We can't go into Maryland playing like that. We have some tough teams coming down the road. We needed this as a little wake-up call. They're a scrappy bunch. Their record doesn't show how good those guys are. We knew we were going to get their best game. We get everyone's best game. We bend, but we don't break. We know what kind of defense we have. We've just got to clean up the mistakes. We can't continue to play like that down the stretch. I feel like we got a little bit lax once we put a lot of points on the board and once they started chipping away slowly but surely, but you can't get like that. You've got to keep the pressure on them always, and that's something with us, though. The coaches had a great gameplan for us and putting us in spots we could excel, but we can't take our foot off the gas pedal."

Peppers had one of the more memorable moments of the Michigan State game. He picked up the Spartans' busted two-point conversion attempt and sprinted 98 yards down the MSU sideline for the two points. He broke the goal line like a sprinter breaking the tape. "How's Peppers not the fastest guy?" Harbaugh said. "I thought I heard a sonic boom on that two-point conversion. I've seen it at practice so many times. Whoa, that is so fast. Someday he'll go to the Combine and run a 40 time, and it will be so interesting to see what he runs. That's going to be in the 4.3s somewhere. When he picked up that loose option pitch and was running down, I thought I heard a sonic boom. I was a little disappointed parachutes didn't come out. It just looked like what was going to happen. I thought when he got to the goal line, I thought some parachutes were going to come out. Impressive, Impressive. Mercy!"

Even though he did a backflip at the end of the game, it was his sprint toward the goal line that turned most heads. Peppers skidded at the back of the end zone and wound up on his back. "At first I wasn't trying to run fast, but then I heard somebody behind me," Pepper said. "I'm like, 'Okay, stop trying to be pretty, just get the ball in the end zone, and put it out of reach.' I slipped at the end, and it messed it all up."

By the end of the game, Harbaugh was regaled by one particular chant that could be heard ringing throughout Spartan Stadium. It very clearly was: "Fuck Jim Harbaugh!" And the Spartan fans showered him with it. Harbaugh had a great time with it. There is no love lost between Michigan State and Michigan fans, and he absolutely knew what they were saying, but he twisted it and laughed about it. "I heard it, I heard it," Harbaugh said very enthusiastically on his weekly Monday night radio show. "And I thought it was really great, classy. I thought they were saying, 'Love Jim Harbaugh,' and they kept repeating it. 'Love Jim Harbaugh! Love Jim Harbaugh!' I thought, *That's great sportsmanship here by the Michigan State Spartans.* The next day I read ESPN. They were saying, I guess it was 'Frick Jim Harbaugh.' I guess I have to get my hearing checked. I could have sworn they were saying, 'Love Jim Harbaugh!'"

Players from both Michigan and Michigan State are very much

about taking possession of the Paul Bunyan Trophy. It was presented for the first time in the 1953 meeting and was first presented by Michigan governor G. Mennen Williams to commemorate the Spartans joining the Big Ten. It is a four-foot wooden statue of the legendary Paul Bunyan astride an axe with his feet planted on a map of the state of Michigan. Two flags—one with the Michigan "M" and the other with the Spartan "S"—are planted on either side of Bunyan, who stands atop a five-foot stand.

Several Michigan players were looking to take the Paul Bunyan Trophy back from Michigan State on the field, but Paul was nowhere to be found. This drew some outrage from Lewis and also on social media, but the trophy was waiting in the Michigan locker room, as has been tradition. According to *Forty Years in the Big House* by Jon Falk, who had been the longtime Michigan equipment manager, Michigan has always celebrated Paul Bunyan as a team in the locker room, just as they did last Saturday.

Falk, who travels with the team and is a bit of an advisor to Harbaugh, wrote that it had always been the tradition of both teams to make it a locker room trophy. But in 2008 before the game, the Michigan State equipment manager told Falk that if MSU won, he wanted the trophy presented on the field. "Something Michigan would never do," Falk said.

Since that season the Spartans, who had won seven of the last eight rivalry games before Michigan's victory, had celebrated with Paul on the field. Falk retrieved the trophy on Saturday from the MSU locker room, so that it could be moved to Michigan's locker room where the players could celebrate with it and take photos and selfies. "I had to kiss him right on the lips real hard, real good, real deep as well," nose tackle Ryan Glasgow deadpanned. "We're really glad to have him back."

It's just a trophy, but Harbaugh has always told them that winning every available trophy should always be a goal. "This is what we worked so hard for in the offseason," offensive guard Kyle

Kalis told MGoBlue.com. "This was our goal coming in to get Paul back home, and we succeeded. I saw him and gave him a nice long, hard stare. I gave him a hug and passed him along."

The Paul Bunyan Trophy is not a thing of beauty. Falk, who had always watched over both Paul and the Little Brown Jug, said that while it isn't attractive, it had improved with age. Perhaps absence makes the heart grow fonder. "The longer we're away from him, the prettier he looks," Falk said. "And yesterday, Paul Bunyan was the prettiest person in the locker room. We have missed him. To have Paul back at Michigan is a big deal."

Harbaugh had a trophy case built in the Michigan locker room to hold the Little Brown Jug, which goes to the winner of the Michigan-Minnesota game, and Paul Bunyan, which is where Paul will live until the next game. That way the players see the trophies every day they're in the locker room. Harbaugh uses anything and everything for motivation. "We came in here expecting to get it back," Wilton Speight said. "It wasn't like a surprise."

Peppers admitted there was a sense of relief to finally win the trophy. "Ah, man, it's been a long time coming," Peppers said. "Last year I heard they already put him in the [Michigan] locker room, and then that crazy play happened. But now he's coming back to AA. We're each going to get our own little Paul Bunyan Trophies. I can't wait. It was an exhilarating feeling to finally get this chip off our shoulder. This one we had marked since last year. We just wanted to come in here and bring Paul back."

It was love at first sight for the players when they saw the Paul Bunyan Trophy in the locker room. But that shouldn't have come as a surprise. As Harbaugh said, that's the absolute best kind of love.

15

Poll Position

Jack Harbaugh has been a lifelong Cleveland Indians fan, so the World Series was of particular interest. He had attended a game early in the season with Tom Crean, his son-in-law and the then-Indiana basketball coach. Jack was excited about the possibilities of seeing his Indians win it all.

And then...on Sunday night before Michigan's week of preparation would begin for Maryland, there was Jim Harbaugh; wife, Sarah; and his parents, Jack and Jackie, sitting in the Wrigley Field bleachers in left field. Harbaugh was introduced, and there were some boos, apparently because of neighboring fans of Notre Dame and other Big Ten schools. Wearing a blue Jumpman Michigan hoodie, he and Sarah wore the standard blue Cubs hat. He also wore his glove, which has always been standard practice for Harbaugh when he has attended ballgames. His father Jack wore a Michigan hat to the game.

The four drove to Chicago that day. "The trip over was tremendous," he said. "We had the windows rolled up, the radio turned off, the cell phones put away. We were telling stories and laughing and sharing. An amazing part of a signature evening." But a Cubs hat? What about rooting for the Indians in support of his father? "Definitely I find myself Cubs, Cubs, Cubs," Harbaugh said. "I'm with Greg Mattison rooting for the Cubs."

Harbaugh, who had thrown the first pitch at a Detroit Tigers game the previous summer, had thrown out the first pitch of a Cubs game that summer in July. "We had a great time. It was a tremendous atmosphere," Harbaugh said. "It was one of those signature moments being at a World Series game with my dad; my mom; and my wife,

Sarah. It was outstanding. He's been very excited. It means a lot to him. It's real."

Harbaugh had often said he wanted to be a major leaguer when he was growing up and loved the World Series experience. "It's a little bit like ice cream, though," he said. "It's so good. It's good to be back to football. Football you could do every day. Baseball is almost too much fun. Like ice cream, you couldn't eat every day."

After indicating he would be rooting all the way for the Cubs, he also listed his favorite teams in order. "I really love the A's, love the Tigers, Cubs for me, got feeling for the Pittsburgh Pirates, and also the Arizona Diamondbacks, and Cleveland Indians, and the San Francisco Giants," he said. "There's an order there. I have several favorites."

But the fact Harbaugh had taken his glove to the game seemed to be the thing most gravitated to and discussed. In a Father's Day story that appeared in *The Detroit News* in 2015, Jack Harbaugh said Jim has always brought a baseball glove to games. "He brings a glove and he will insist on sitting somewhere where there are no obstructions, so when the ball is hit, there's no screen it can go into," Jack said. "If it's hit at his section, he wants a clean shot at it. He claims he has 19 balls he's gotten at the games and he claims they aren't batting practice balls, but ones he got during the games at some point during the nine innings. The ball comes, no matter who's around him, it's everyone for themselves. He will dive for the ball. He will get on the concrete and crawl on his hands and knees to retrieve the ball. We did this at San Francisco last year at the Giants game. A couple people behind us weren't as aggressive for the ball, and we had to apologize that [Jim] works on a different frequency."

Speaking of different frequencies, Harbaugh and Maryland coach D.J. Durkin are both guilty of that. It would be the first time the two coached against each other since Durkin left after one season as Michigan's defensive coordinator to take over the Terps. Durkin also had worked for Harbaugh at Stanford. Maryland had started the season strong, and Harbaugh said he would always root for Maryland except this one weekend. The Terps were one win from bowl eligibility (5–3, 2–3 Big Ten) while second-ranked Michigan (8–0, 5–0 Big Ten) was No. 3 in the College Football Playoff rankings. "Obviously, our teams are playing each other this weekend, but it's the players who are playing each other—not he and I," Durkin said on the Big Ten conference call that week, reciting a line similar to one Harbaugh had used many times.

The Terps, who were in disarray after the 2015 season, won their first four games but then they had lost three of four games heading into Ann Arbor. "He's done a fabulous job," Harbaugh said, "always respected D.J. as a tremendous competitor at the highest level. I smile when I think about his competitiveness, always happy for a friend's success. You see the energy, you see the strength, you see the competitiveness, execution on the field. On the flip side, this will be a championship game, a real test for our club."

Harbaugh said it's a thrill to see his assistant coaches move on to bigger roles. That's always the objective in his mind—to help his assistants develop to a point that teams with head coaching vacancies come calling. "I follow all the coaches we worked with and pull for them when they're not playing us," Harbaugh said. "Happy for the other guy's success. Personally, I like it a lot. Professionally, I see guys develop, reach their goals, especially when you know going in what their goals are. You want to see your friends have success. He goes all out, does things at a very high level. A lot of enthusiasm, kindred spirit, very happy for him."

The Michigan defensive players said they are looking forward to seeing Durkin again. He is one who matches Harbaugh's intensity, and both have been described as tornados, active, spinning, and just constantly going, going, going. Running back Karan Higdon said it's hard to decide who is more intense. "That's a close call," Higdon said. "I don't know. Coach Harbaugh can be very, very intense, and Coach Durkin can be very, very intense. They're both masterminds of their domain. It's a hard decision."

Heading into the game, Durkin said he had a bit of an advantage not present during preparations for other games because he knew the defensive personnel and had a good sense for how offensive coordinator Tim Drevno runs the offense. "Familiarity definitely helps," Durkin said. "It's less time spent on identifying who's who personnel-wise and what they can or can't do and the strengths and weakness, which is something you go through every week when you're gameplanning a team. That process is a little different when you're playing a team you're very familiar with their personnel. It's more about what our players know about their personnel and how they execute. There certainly are some benefits to it, but it comes down to the players and their preparation."

This would also be the first week of the College Football Poll, and the Wolverines were projected to be No. 3 by most experts, including ESPN college football analysts Joey Galloway and David Pollack. The two appeared on an ESPN conference call that Monday morning to advance the network's exclusive coverage of the College Football Playoff Selection Committee's weekly rankings and they both believed the rankings would be revealed in this order: Alabama, Clemson, Michigan, and Washington. "If you look at the Big Ten right now, Michigan looks to be the best team in the Big Ten," Galloway said. "That is a surprise. I thought they were maybe a year away from being that, but right now they look like the best team and the favorite to win the Big Ten and the favorite to represent the Big Ten in the playoff. That part of it is a surprise. What [Harbaugh's] been able to do with Wilton Speight, coming into the season, nobody knew who their quarterback was going to be, and now we look at Wilton Speight as a guy who has developed into a playmaker with the ability to go down field. That makes this offense a much different threat. We knew they'd be physical. We knew they'd go two tight ends and run the ball between tackles, we knew they'd go play-action pass with their tight ends, but now the ability to go downfield makes Michigan a scary type of offense to go against. That part of it is a surprise."

Pollack said Harbaugh had made the Wolverines relevant again in less than two seasons and he was not surprised by their presence in the national playoff conversation. "He's worth every penny," Pollack said. "Whatever it takes to get a guy like that because now the whole offseason you're talking about Michigan. Recruits are talking about Michigan. Ann Arbor is now a place that's sexy again. He's done an amazing job offensively. The defense was already good. The defense was already set up to be successful. They had guys on D that were tough and physical. But now you've seen the offense start to take shape with him. You see him using a fullback and you see him using tight ends and play-action. And you've seen Speight kind of grow up, too, and his toughness and his ability to hang in there and take shots and understand where to go with the football. So I don't think anybody is surprised Michigan is back. Everybody saw them being more of a player."

Michigan had four remaining regular-season games starting with Maryland at Michigan Stadium and then the Wolverines would travel to inconsistent Iowa for a night game, return home to face Indiana, and then face Ohio State in Columbus. Pollack, like Galloway, also saw Michigan as the Big Ten favorite at this point in the season—even with those games at Iowa and Ohio State looming. "I feel a lot more comfortable and I feel a lot better about Michigan now that I've seen Ohio State," Pollack said. "I think they're looking even better with that matchup with Ohio State. At the beginning of the season when they were spreading the ball around and playing good D and the offense was really clicking and humming, I thought this was a team that could beat Michigan pretty easily. Now, you start looking at it like, Michigan's defensive line is obviously a lot better than Penn State, and Penn State handled Ohio State up front. I think it's actually going to be a heck of a showdown. I think that game is going to be really good."

Michigan was coming off a victory at Michigan State last Saturday to remain unbeaten, which is exactly where Galloway thought the Wolverines would be. "I'm not surprised at all they're sitting at 8–0," Galloway said. "We all looked at their schedule before the season began. Everyone thought the first half of their schedule was very soft, even though Wisconsin has sort of come out of nowhere and surprised a lot of people, and that has now become a good win. Colorado is becoming a pretty good team that's surprised people, and now that is a good win. We all thought they would go through the first half of their schedule pretty easily."

Most of the Michigan players were only mildly curious about the playoff rankings. They said it was fun to be part of the conversation but also saw the danger of allowing it to potentially cloud their judgment and cause them to lose focus. Receiver Amara Darboh planned to watch the unveiling but made clear that nothing matters until the final poll. At this stage they knew they still had four games to go. So what would be the point of getting distracted by it? Harbaugh said he would take a peek at the College Football Playoff rankings when they'd be revealed on television, but that would be the extent of his interest.

This would be the first of five rankings made by the College Football Playoff Committee. The four playoff teams would be announced December 4. To this point Michigan was one of five unbeaten teams and ranked No. 2 in the AP and Coaches' polls, but those do not factor into the College Football Playoff rankings. "I'm not going to be able to work that into our preparations for Maryland," Harbaugh said when asked if he planned to watch the show. "We'll be doing other things. Not to say we don't check them, it takes about 15 seconds to check and see where you are. We aspire to be as good as we can be. That's the simple part of it."

Harbaugh said watching the show would take a "backseat" to watching Maryland tape and gameplanning. The Wolverines, newly minted at No. 3 in the playoff rankings, pummeled Maryland

59–3, and Harbaugh wasted no time in the postgame locker room reminding his players of reality. Harbaugh told the team about being on Michigan's team in 1985 that was ranked No. 2 when it traveled to face No. 1 Iowa in 1985. The Hawkeyes won 12–10. Michigan finished 10–1–1 that season, played in the Fiesta Bowl, and was ranked No. 2 in the final poll.

His message to his players could not have been more clear. "You can't take that for granted because you never know what can be taken from you," fullback Khalid Hill said after the Maryland victory. "He told us it happened before, so don't think we've made it. We haven't made it yet."

The players have had constant reminders this season about what it takes to achieve their goals. Tom Brady and Michael Jordan stopped by. Legendary major leaguer Hank Aaron had spoken to the team a few weeks earlier, and former Michigan quarterback Brian Griese, who led the Wolverines to an unbeaten season in 1997 and a share of the national championship, visited with the players that last week.

Their messages resonated with the players. "Hank Aaron said there's really no secret to success. It just comes down to hard work," Jake Butt said. "Since we walked off the field last year against Florida, we've had that mentality. We knew what this team could be. Through winter conditioning, summer conditioning, fall camp, every single week this season so far, we've had that mentality, that lunch-pail mentality, just hard work because we don't want to let this opportunity slip through our fingers. These kind of opportunities don't come around every single year when you're undefeated and you're playing good football. We're not going to take that for granted. We're not going to relax a little bit. We're not going to start patting ourselves on the back. If anything, we're going to work even harder going forward because we know how much is on the line."

Quarterback Wilton Speight said the team now approached the final stretch as if it was the NCAA Men's Basketball Tournament.

"It's championship week, and we take that to heart," Speight said. "We know it's really win or go home at this point. All this means nothing if we're 9–1 this time next week [after Iowa]."

Griese asked the players if they felt they had accomplished anything yet. Some hesitated, Speight said, wondering if the correct answer was "No." "But he was the one who said, 'Of course you have accomplished stuff. You're 8–0, you're trying to get to 9–0, and you put yourself in good position,'" Speight said. "It's rewarding, but there's a lot more to do. We've just got to figure how to keep it going."

With Maryland already in the rearview mirror, the Wolverines already were thinking about the upcoming game at Iowa, the second game of the season they would play at night. Kinnick Stadium already is an intimidating place to play during the day, but a night game there adds another dimension of difficulty.

The Wolverines previously had destroyed Rutgers in a night game in unpleasant rainy conditions, and the early forecast for Iowa City the following week was clear with a low of 35 degrees. "My initial thought is I hope global warming keeps it up," Speight said. "It's a night game at Iowa, and that's going to be brutal if it's cold, the wind chill and the wind. I know they're going to be focused. They're an extremely well-coached team, very fundamentally sound, a lot like Wisconsin."

Weather aside, the players got the message from Harbaugh after Maryland. He wanted them to stay on edge, understanding that anything could happen from here on out. That would be their focus going forward. "We're always uncomfortable," Hill said. "Any team could beat us on any given day. Going into [Michigan] State, I'm thinking, *Oh, we've got to be really on our stuff because this could be the one.* You never know when you're unbeaten, which team could be the team. You've seen it plenty of times before. You've got to go in each week as a championship game."

16

Animation and Adversity

O N THE SUNDAY NIGHT BEFORE IOWA WEEK, JIM Harbaugh was featured prominently in dialogue from the animated show, *The Simpsons*. Homer Simpson called Marge Simpson after a lacrosse game. "Kirk is like a sports genius who everybody hates," Homer told her.

"Worse than Jim Harbaugh?" Marge said.

Priceless.

And Harbaugh thought so, too. During his Monday night radio show, he laughed about the mention, made clear he found it to be a sort of badge of honor, and then shared who he considers his favorite animated character. "You know, people have been making sport of me for ever since I can remember. My earliest memories, five, six, seven, in the schoolyard," Harbaugh said, "just my whole life, they make sport of me. But it's pretty high class—*The Simpsons*! It's one of my favorite shows. The animated shows, *The Simpsons* and *SpongeBob* are two of my all-time favorites."

SpongeBob is someone to whom Harbaugh relates. That's right. He relates to an animated television character. "I love his attitude," Harbaugh said. "He attacks each day with an enthusiasm unknown to mankind. What a great employee he is. He's a go-getter. He's always got a bounce in his step. He's got pizazz."

During a graduation speech at Paramus Catholic in New Jersey in June, Harbaugh even referenced SpongeBob SquarePants. He asked the crowd if they'd rather be SpongeBob—energetic and optimistic and always attacking the day as Harbaugh does—or would they rather be Squidward, the arrogant octopus.

Harbaugh also revealed he is a big fan of *The Simpsons* and said he happens to be a Homer fan.

A day after *The Simpsons* poked good-natured fun at Harbaugh, he was front and center at president Barack Obama's speech at a Hillary Clinton rally at the university's baseball stadium. This was not Harbaugh's first encounter with the president, not by a longshot. Earlier in the year, Harbaugh and his wife were guests at a State of the Union address, and the previous year he had made a trip to the White House in part because Harbaugh was working with First Lady Obama on her "Reach Higher" education initiative.

The president and Harbaugh spoke briefly but long enough for Obama to ask for a Michigan football sweatsuit to take to the golf course. Harbaugh said it would be in the mail immediately. Since it was a game week and Michigan was preparing to take its unblemished record on the road to Iowa for a night game, Obama made certain to reference the Wolverines and did mention Michigan's 9–0 football record before making his remarks. "He's a great guy," Harbaugh said. "I thought it was tremendous he gave our team a shout-out. That was neat. The president of the United States mentions the football team you're part of, that's pretty neat."

Although Harbaugh had made it clear to his players that he encourages open discussion about any topics and wants them to feel free to share their opinions, he did not plan to talk to them as a group about the presidential election. He did meet individually with players who wanted to discuss the election. "No, I haven't made a dramatic plea to get out to vote," Harbaugh said. "I was in the vicinity with maybe 10,000 other Michigan people, many students [at the rally]. You've got to think a student that attends a speech of the president of the United States, the leader of the free world, that's something that's going to be a signature moment in their educational experience at the University of Michigan and in their college career."

Receiver Jehu Chesson attended the rally, as did Harbaugh's son, James Harbaugh Jr., a Michigan sophomore. Young Harbaugh waited in line Sunday for a ticket and arrived in the wee hours

Jim Harbaugh throws a pass to Tom Brady, who served as Michigan's honorary captain for the Colorado game, prior to Michigan's 45–28 victory at The Big House. (USA TODAY Sports Images)

Jim Harbaugh relished his game of catch with Tom Brady, saying it ranked up there with catching passes from his father, Jack Harbaugh. (USA TODAY Sports Images)

*Wide receiver Amara Darboh catches the game-winning, 46-yard touchdown pass in the fourth quarter to help Michigan defeat Wisconsin 14–7. (*USA TODAY *Sports Images)*

Heisman Trophy finalist Jabrill Peppers scores a first-half touchdown against Michigan State. The All-American also returned a two-point conversion, made seven tackles, and had a sack in the 32–23 victory. (AP Images)

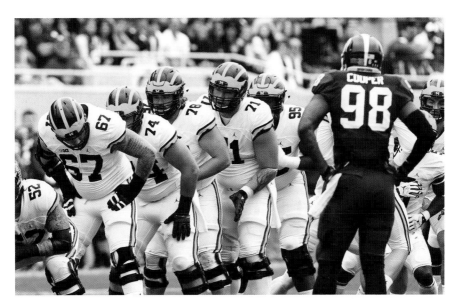

Against rival Michigan State, Michigan uses its "Train" formation, which the Wolverines had unveiled against Wisconsin. (AP Images)

During a blizzard at The Big House, the Michigan offensive line heads for the sideline during the penultimate game of the 2016 regular season. (AP Images)

Linebacker Devin Bush (left) and defensive tackle Michael Dwumfour (right) make snow angels after defeating Indiana 20–10 in the final home game of the 2016 season. (AP Images)

Michigan defenders, including Jabrill Peppers (No. 5) and Delano Hill (No. 44), converge on Ohio State quarterback J.T. Barrett during the hard-fought, double-overtime game. (AP Images)

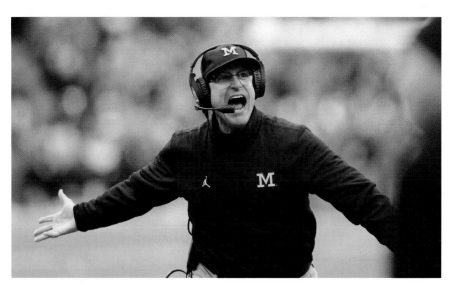

Jim Harbaugh reacts to one of the many questionable officiating calls during Michigan's 30–27 loss to rival Ohio State. (USA TODAY Sports Images)

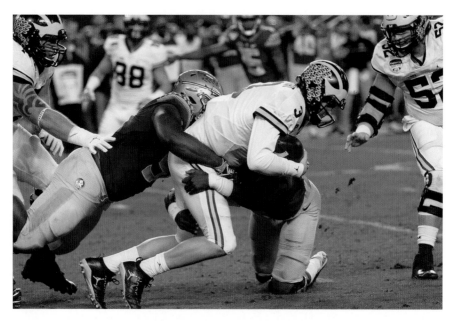

During the Orange Bowl, the Florida State defense pummels Michigan quarterback Wilton Speight, who called the Seminoles' defensive line the best he faced all season. (AP Images)

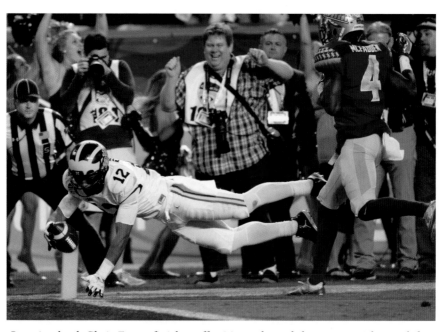

Running back Chris Evans finishes off a 30-yard touchdown run with 1:57 left in the Orange Bowl to give Michigan a 30–27 lead, which it would relinquish. (AP Images)

Anxious to take the field in 2016, the Wolverines have seen their program restored under Jim Harbaugh's watch. (USA TODAY Sports Images)

Defensive lineman Rashan Gary, a prized recruit and a major contributor during the 2016 season, likely will anchor the defense for years to come. (AP Images)

Monday to be part of the crowd. Jim Harbaugh sat with athletic director Warde Manuel. "They're literally feet, yards from where we practice at Schembechler Hall," Harbaugh said. "The leader of the free world is in our vicinity. That's pretty cool."

The Simpsons and a presidential rally aside, this was an important week and test for the Wolverines. For quarterback Wilton Speight, it was a time of revelation. The young quarterback—who had felt the wrath of Harbaugh in the spring of 2015, captured for all eternity on an HBO special—was ready to pack up and leave at the time.

Now, confident as the starter, leading the Big Ten in pass efficiency, and feeling good about Michigan's chances—with the Wolverines ranked No. 3 in the College Football Playoff—he also had the confidence to share how tough it was for him early in the transition to Harbaugh. Speight was buried on the depth chart in the spring of Harbaugh's first year. During an HBO special, Harbaugh was caught yelling at a quarterback whose jersey number was blurred. It was a very tall quarterback, though, who obviously was Speight. "If you want to look at me with that look, go fucking somewhere else," Harbaugh told Speight as captured by HBO.

Speight almost did and had his father start searching for other options. "That redshirt freshman fall camp, I was on the phone with my parents. [I] basically was, 'Okay, I'm out. Let's find a different school,'" Speight said. "They were on board. They obviously wanted me to stay here, but they were going to support my decision. One morning I just woke up and was about to tell Coach and I just, I don't know, didn't feel right. So I said I'll give it another week and I started playing better and by the end of camp I was taking reps with the twos."

It finally got to the point Speight could joke frequently about his HBO debut. "Everyone saw the HBO special," Speight said. "That wasn't exactly the bubbly, 'Hey, stick around.' That was more, 'Please get out of my face and never come back.' Coach Harbaugh told me over the summer when we had our individual meetings, 'Hey, you're

going to get a shot,' so I believed him. I started to see the writing on the wall a little bit the first week of camp. I said screw it. I'm going to work as hard as I can."

The funny thing is, Harbaugh had experienced a similar situation during his playing days at Michigan. He, too, considered transferring before he got the starting quarterback job his junior season. When Harbaugh read Speight's comments about nearly packing up and moving on, he was reminded of his career at Michigan under an equally demanding coach, Bo Schembechler. "I thought there was a time where I wasn't going to play at Michigan and was told that and called my dad," Harbaugh said on his weekly radio appearance in Detroit. "It was like déjà vu, reading what Wilton was saying. That happened to me my sophomore year."

After redshirting his first season, Harbaugh barely played as a sophomore. During his redshirt sophomore year in 1984, Harbaugh played well, but he broke his arm in the Michigan State game at the midway point of the season and was sidelined. He then led the Wolverines to a No. 2 ranking in 1985 and had great success in 1986, beating Ohio State and winning the Big Ten title to play in the Rose Bowl. Harbaugh learned an important lesson, as did Speight. Sticking out a tough situation often can be the best way to deal with a difficult situation. It makes you work harder if you realize this is what you want to be devoted to accomplishing. "Tom Brady, I bet he had a few of those thoughts," Harbaugh said of the former Michigan quarterback who went on to win five Super Bowls with the New England Patriots. "It's a great lesson. You don't want to quit. You don't want to take a knee too early."

Harbaugh laughed a bit after the Maryland game when he said Speight should be in the Heisman Trophy conversation. While highly unlikely that Speight woud be considered, Harbaugh put it out there probably with the intention of giving Speight added confidence. Pretty much every time Harbaugh is asked to make a comparison, he declines. He doesn't like to do that. He also doesn't

like to set boundaries or specific expectations, but Speight had impressed him. "Yeah, he's superseding the hopes," Harbaugh said. "He's gone past what we were hoping he would be in a big way. He's been outstanding. I'd be lying if I said he hasn't more than exceeded what we were even hoping he could be. Young player having his first college starts, you would expect it would be a process. You'd expect there would be a two-step forward, a step back, bumps in the road, tough games, but he's met the challenge at every task, acquitted himself more than really good. Keep going.

"He's got a hot hand, but it's come through preparation and come through being really important to him. It's really why you don't put expectations on people. It's why you don't limit what you think they can be. You let them have at it, and that's been our approach with every position. If you put expectations on somebody or limit them, maybe they don't reach as high as they possibly can."

With Speight playing at a high level and the defense setting a tone, Ryan Glasgow said the team was getting more physical with its goals in sight. "We go out there with no ill will or malicious intent," he said. "We're taught to play physical. We're taught to tackle and we're taught to run through hits. Our goal is to win the Big Ten championship. We have a real shot, and I think we have a great chance of doing it. If we lose a game—Wilton had wise words the other day—he said we didn't come this far just to come this far. We have bigger goals in mind."

In Harbaugh's only appearance as a player at Kinnick Stadium in 1985, No. 1 Iowa defeated No. 2 Michigan 12–10 on a last-second field goal. If he remembered anything about that game, he wasn't interested in sharing it early in the week on his radio show. What he did recollect was the visitors' pink locker room, which former Iowa coach Hayden Fry decided would be a soothing color for the visitors and would make them less fierce. Bo Schembechler had Jon Falk and his equipment staff cover the walls with butcher's paper, but the sinks also were pink. "They couldn't put paper over those,"

Harbaugh said.

When the Wolverines stepped into the locker room at Iowa that Saturday night, they felt at home. The walls were covered with custom Michigan wallpaper with photos of the current team. It took hours for the equipment staff to get it done, but the redecorating was quite impressive.

But making the Michigan players feel at home in the locker room didn't quite carry over to the field. The Wolverines were upset by unranked Iowa and saw their unbeaten season evaporate when Keith Duncan made a 33-yard field goal with no time left. The Kinnick Stadium field was then overtaken by a mass of Iowa fans. Even so, Michigan (9–1, 6–1 Big Ten) was still in the Big Ten championship and playoff mix. If the Wolverines could win their final two games—at home against Indiana and then at Ohio State in the final regular-season game—their goals remained a reality.

It was an interesting day of football in terms of the big national picture. The Wolverines were one of three top four College Football Playoff teams to lose that Saturday. Only Alabama won. No. 2 Clemson and No. 4 Washington also lost. No. 5 Ohio State routed Maryland, and No. 6 Louisville beat Wake Forest. The next several teams had two losses, so Michigan was in a large one-loss pool. "We were treating every week like a championship week, and that was ultimately our goal—to finish the season undefeated," Speight said. "We've all been talking, and everything is still right there for us. We just have to handle our business for the remainder of the regular season and then just let it play out. It's all still right there."

Harbaugh was asked about his team's focus. "Every little thing isn't going to go our team's way or anybody's way," Harbaugh said. "Every little thing doesn't always go your way. To win, you have to make it that way. We didn't do enough things to make it that way. They played well. They played hard. They set the edge extremely well, tackled well, had good coverage. We just didn't get it done tonight, didn't do enough to go our way."

The Wolverines, who entered the game averaging 487.4 yards of offense, were held to 201 yards and had two costly turnovers in the game. "We didn't make enough plays to extend drives and convert first downs. We missed some deep throws," Harbaugh said. "Give Iowa credit. They tackled, they blocked, they played a very good football game. Congratulate them and move on."

It was a wild fourth quarter. Kenny Allen made two field goals, including a career-long 51-yarder with 9:35 left in the game to give Michigan a slim, 13–10 lead. Michigan got the ball right back, and, just as it looked like the Wolverines were driving for another score, Speight was intercepted on a third-and-9 throw. Iowa's Manny Rugamba yanked the ball away from Jehu Chesson for the interception, giving the Hawkeyes the ball at their 25-yard line with 3:43 left.

But on first down, Iowa quarterback C.J. Beathard threw deep and was intercepted by Channing Stribling for the defensive back's fourth pick of the season. Michigan got the ball at its 16-yard line with 1:54 left. Iowa had three timeouts, and the Wolverines could not get a first down and were forced to punt. "Nothing we can do about it now," Michigan safety Dymonte Thomas said. "There's no point of sitting here and saying this and that, what we could have done, or should have done. All we can control is the future, so that's all we're going to focus on."

What Michigan would have to focus on shortly after the game was the health and future playing availability of Speight. His left shoulder was injured with about four and a half minutes left in the fourth quarter when he took off and scrambled on second and 12. He was tackled by two Iowa players, and one laid on top of him. When Speight got up, he began uncomfortably moving his left arm. On third down he made the pass to Chesson that was intercepted. On the sideline Speight was examined by doctors who tried to locate the injury by feeling the shoulder area under the pads. Speight returned for the final series.

Feeling less than his best but also not appearing to be injured, Speight did meet with the media after the game. "We're not chipper. It stings," he said. "Hey, it's life. It's football. We'll figure it out and figure out a way to get in the win column next week."

Harbaugh's message in the postgame locker room was clear to the players. "If we keep winning, the rest will take care of itself," Jake Butt said.

Perhaps, though, this is where having five straight home games and not having much experience playing out of state—this was the second trip out of Michigan for the Wolverines—caught up to them. Iowa is among the most challenging stadiums in which to play because of the tight sideline and the fact the fans are on top of the visitors' sideline and are well-versed in slinging insults.

By no means, the Wolverines said, did they take the Hawkeyes (6–4) lightly. "That never crossed any of our minds," Speight said. "Coming to Iowa, it doesn't matter how they had been playing before. We get everyone's best shot. Being who we are, and the coaches we have, the attention we bring, it's championship week for us, but it's literally everyone's championship game when they play the Michigan Wolverines. We knew it was going to be a hostile crowd and we were going to take their best shot, and they got the better of it."

He said the team would approach the loss as it does a win. The Wolverines would move on quickly. "It will be behind us, just like a win," Speight said. "We enjoy the wins for a couple hours. We'll be pissed off about this, mourn this a little bit, and just like a win, it's on to Indiana and put it behind us."

The team never looked at possible scenarios if they were to lose. "Before tonight we didn't really look at it, 'Okay, we have some margin of error,'" Speight said. "It happened, so now we say, 'Everything is fine, we're going to move on, and if we win out, we'll be okay.' But it was never, 'Okay, we have one slip up and we do that, it's all right.' That was never our mind-set."

The Wolverines, who had won their first nine games of the season and 10 including the New Year's Day bowl game, were certain they would rebound from the loss. "We're going to bounce back," Thomas said. "We worked really hard in the offseason. We know if we win out what lies ahead of us. So we're going to get back to work Monday and take care of Indiana and take care of Ohio State."

The seniors were confident they would find a way to return to their winning ways, in part because they believed Harbaugh would devise a plan to do so but also because the players had all worked so hard together in the offseason when the spine of a team is developed. "I've played with these guys for pretty much four years. But the thing is, I just know how these guys respond," Butt said. "I worked with them in the offseason, I've worked with them in the spring, and I know they're hard-working guys, and I know we're going to be eager to get back to work. I know my teammates and I trust them, and we're just ready to get to work."

But time would tell how seriously injured Speight was and if he would be able to play going forward with so much on the line.

17

Reflecting on Bo

F OR THE FIRST TIME ALL SEASON, JIM HARBAUGH HAD to coach this team coming off a loss, and the players had to respond and rebound. Harbaugh's message after losing at Iowa was to "soldier up" and keep preparing as they had all season, approaching week after week as a "championship week" because getting to the Big Ten Championship Game was still there for them. Win the next two games, starting against Indiana in the final regular-season home game and the final home game for the seniors, and everything was still on the table. "Four years?" senior tight end Jake Butt said. "It's hard to sum it up in even one or two sentences. You look back on it and see some of the ups and downs and the things I've been through and we've been through as a team. It's unbelievable."

Sentiments aside, Butt said the team would learn from the loss and make amends against Indiana. "It's a game we could have won, so that's going to sting a little bit," he said at the start of the game week. "We remind ourselves and each other that everything we set out for at the beginning of the season is still right in front of us. We're going to learn from this loss and become tougher and better because of it. We control our destiny, so as long as we keep handling business we're not worried about what anybody is doing. We just have to handle our own business, and the rest will take care of itself. There's no panic button. We're not going to let one loss turn into two. We're going to continue with the same mentality, get back to work today, and move forward. It's really the only way to go about this. I'm very confident in our team to be able to bounce back from something like this. It starts with our coaching staff. They're going to put us in a position to succeed. We're going to lay it all on the line and leave it all on the field this weekend and going forward. I have full confidence in everybody on the team."

If Harbaugh knew on Monday of game week—or any of the days heading into the game that Wilton Speight would be able to play after suffering that left shoulder injury late in the Iowa game—he wasn't sharing it with the world. He called it a game-time decision. This would be a blow for the Wolverines, who at 9–1 with two games remaining still had plenty of hope for achieving the lofty goals they had set out to earn. Speight had started every game, completed 62.3 percent of his passes for 2,156 yards, had thrown 15 touchdowns—and run for one—to four interceptions.

With Speight's condition an unknown, backups John O'Korn and Shane Morris would get the majority of the reps in practice. O'Korn had appeared in seven games up to that point and had limited exposure, throwing for 114 yards and two touchdowns. But he had made 16 starts while at Houston and was the American Athletic Conference Rookie of the Year in 2013, so there was plenty of confidence in his skill. "If John's number is called, we're fully confident in him," Butt said. "We've seen what he can do. Since he got here, he's been a hard worker, great note taker, great leader. He's got everything you need to do to get the job done. If his number is called, if it turns out Wilton can't go, he'll be ready to go. We're fully confident in him. Him and Wilton are pretty similar quarterbacks. We're going to be running the same exact plays. John has been doing a great job understanding his role and he's been ready every single week and preparing every single week as if he were the starter. They both put it where it needs to be. They both have great arms, great accuracy. Both are throwing tight spirals. They spin the ball really well. John might rely on his feet a little bit more, as we saw in the spring game. Wilton's a little bit bigger and can stand in the pocket. The name of the game is just find a way to get the job done. Both have done that, can do that, and will do that."

Throughout the week Harbaugh said he would not discuss specifics of Speight's injury but did say that any reports that Speight would be out for the rest of the season were "incorrect," which allowed Michigan fans to breathe a bit easier. The week took a more reflective tone by Thursday. It was the 10th anniversary of Bo Schembechler's passing, and those who knew him best spoke of a man who was larger than life. Schembechler had passed away the day before the legendary game in Columbus, Ohio, in 2006 when Michigan was ranked No. 2 and Ohio State was No. 1.

Dan Dierdorf, a college football Hall of Famer and NFL Hall of Famer who has been around the greats in the game, played on Schembechler's first team at Michigan in 1969. "I've been around a lot of people. I've lived a good life," Dierdorf told *The Detroit News* in a series of vignettes from a variety of people who had been touched by Bo. "I've walked halls with Hall of Famers and I've met movie stars and blah, blah, blah. Bo Schembechler was the most charismatic man I've ever known in my entire life. He could suck the air out of a room. Any player who played for Bo, and don't get me wrong—there have been other coaches who have meant so much to their players—but when someone pushes you and prods you and pushes you through that door to do more than you could ever do, when that happens to you, it's a painful process while it's happening, but when it's over, you're a different person. Bo and I fought while I played. He pushed me through that door, but I went through it very begrudgingly. I was so fortunate as I grew older and every day I appreciated more and more what Bo had done to me. After 13 years in the National Football League, all the good things that happened to me in the NFL, still nothing was as good as it was in Ann Arbor. I never had an experience like I had playing for Bo."

Harbaugh played for Schembechler and long before that was a boy running around the Michigan locker rooms and field while his father, Jack, was an assistant. He had known his coach on so many levels and here he was coaching the team he once led and helped build into one of the nation's top programs.

With longtime equipment manager Jon Falk, who had retired

a few years earlier, back in Schembechler Hall at Harbaugh's request, Harbaugh had another connection, along with his father, to Schembechler. Falk was hired by Schembechler from Miami, Ohio, and—for the players and for Harbaugh—he is a conduit to the past. He had been there 40 years and often was charged with explaining many of the traditions, like the Little Brown Jug and the Paul Bunyan Trophy, to the players. Schembechler would tell Falk to talk to the players and tell them about the Rose Bowl and Michigan tradition.

For Harbaugh, Falk had become a valuable sounding board. He frequently discusses with him the ways Schembechler handled a multitude of situations. On the 10th anniversary of Schembechler's passing, Harbaugh, who frequently says he will not "peel back the onion" to reveal much of himself, said he was wistful and spoke eloquently and at length about his former coach. "I think about Bo most days, almost all the time," Harbaugh said. "Jon Falk is right outside of my office, and he and I are the ones who talk about him the most. And my dad and I. It's almost every day there's a story. Most of the time, I'm doing something, trying to decide something, I'll bounce it off Jon or my dad, anybody who knows Bo. And they'll invariably say, 'Bo had a similar thing and Bo did this.' It's awesome. I wish he was here. I wish I could be going through this with him. How cool would that be?"

Harbaugh said he often wonders what Schembechler would think of the job he was doing at Michigan. "I'd want to know. I'd like to think he would think I was doing a good job," he said. "The thing we all look back on—and I speak for myself—but I'm so thankful, so obliged when I think that to be tested by Bo was the making of my soul, obliged and thankful for the hard service he laid down. It was what he expected and it's what I expected he would do. I expected him to be that way, and he was. The counsel you always got from him, he never led you astray. You knew it would be hard to take the path he told you to take, but you knew you would come out on the right side. It was going to be good for your soul. You knew it was going to be hard, but there were sacrifices that had to be made... and it was going to be good for you. He had a tremendous moral compass. It wasn't going to be the easy way. That's what you're thankful for. That's the way he drove the ship that way, the right way, the best way. Somebody on a ship in the crow's nest, and you were happy he was. You knew the direction [it] was going in, the right direction."

Many of those who played for Schembechler—those who coached with him, and those who know him—said they were changed because of him. "Like every other person that's known him, I've been a follower of him," Harbaugh said. "I aspired to be like him. There's no question about that. He's tested me. I feel like everyone else would feel. He's changed me, he's forged me, and I'm proud of that. I know I can look back and think at times, *What would Bo do in this situation?* Throughout the years and still do today. Would he approve of the way we're doing this? I know if I aspired to be like him, where does that lead it? To all those things he was. It doesn't seem like 10 years because you have so many reminders of him in the way you act yourself and the way we all act. He was a great coach, a great teacher. I've learned so much. You learn so much around him. He's the greatest coach you've ever known and one of the greatest men you'd ever hope to be around. He was great on a different level. You aspire to be good like he was. He's as good as they go, as there ever was, ever will be."

A few days later on gameday, another former Schembechler player made his way to Ann Arbor. Les Miles, fired as head coach earlier in the season by LSU, made his first trek to his alma mater since attending Schembechler's funeral. Miles looked like the most popular man on campus as former teammates and longtime friends shook his hand and embraced him. He had twice been linked as a candidate for the Michigan job but never had the opportunity to coach the Wolverines. He almost looked shocked as he was hounded by fans and friends as he dropped by a tailgate hosted by former Wolverines and close friends, Dick Caldarazzo and John Wangler.

It was a star-studded early afternoon with legendary sports broadcaster Dick Enberg and Pittsburgh Pirates manager Clint Hurdle also visiting for the final home game of the season. But Miles, who spent time Saturday with former Wolverines Dierdorf and Jim Brandstatter and Jim Betts, was the draw. "Coming back is something I will do regularly until I get very busy," said Miles, who also added that he wanted to again be a head coach.

Like Harbaugh two days earlier, Miles became wistful about his old coach. "This is us," he said. "This is who we are—the experience of Michigan, the experience of football, and the experience of Bo and Michigan football."

And like so many of the former Michigan players, Miles, who had spoken to Harbaugh earlier that day, praised the job he had done in two seasons. "He's doing just what we want him to," Miles said. "And I say 'we' collectively as a bunch of people who love Michigan."

The first half of the Indiana game was largely forgettable. O'Korn started and played through difficult weather conditions. He struggled to get the offense going. It took senior running back De'Veon Smith, who had a career best day with 158 yards and two long rushing touchdowns in the second half in his final home game, to give the Wolverines a lift in the 20–10 victory.

It was, however, a magical setting late in the game and almost seemed as though Michigan Stadium was encased in a snow globe someone kept shaking. The snow swirled around the stadium, covered the field, and made it difficult to make out the players. Michigan's cheerleaders used a timeout to make snow angels on the corner of the field, and "Let It Snow" played throughout the stadium with the fans singing along: "let it snow, let it snow, let it snow."

After the game the Michigan players ran and slid across the snow, as some took belly dives, and others made enormous snow angels. "Playing in the cold was a lot of fun," O'Korn said after the game. "It was like a scene from a movie or from a dream."

Harbaugh heaped praise on O'Korn and said not only did he have to help the Wolverines beat Indiana, but also the elements. Many think playing football in Michigan means very cold Novembers and snow. Although it is frequently chilly by that time of the season—it actually reached 70 degrees the day before the Michigan-Indiana game—it rarely snows. Linebacker Mike McCray, who grew up in southwestern Ohio, had never played in snowy conditions before.

And like his teammates, he loved it. "I think most of us dreamed of playing in the snow in an actual game," McCray said. "Basically a dream come true, I guess."

It was a dream-like setting for the fans, too, as the "Beat Ohio!" chants could be heard through the falling snow after the Wolverines had beaten the Hoosiers to improve to 10–1, heading into the biggest week of the regular season—the one leading up to Michigan-Ohio State. Outside the stadium as the fans headed out, the "Beat Ohio" chants remained steady and loud. "Now it's finally here. We can zero in on it and put all our focus toward it because this one is all for the marbles," Jabrill Peppers said. "Everything we want is right in front of us. We've just got to go out and execute. It's us and them. The winner probably earns their spot in the College Football Playoff."

Michigan had not won a Big Ten title since 2004 and also has not won in Columbus since 2000. Ohio State had won 13 of the last 15 games against Michigan and four straight. But the Wolverines had to get past Indiana first, and Harbaugh made sure they were not looking ahead. He had called most Saturdays a championship game and now he had the players embracing a win-or-go-home approach these last few weeks. He called them playoff games. "Winning this game feels like one of the best wins I've ever been involved with because it was a playoff game," Harbaugh said. "It was beating a tough Indiana team, and we have a lot of respect for them. They're a heck of a football team. And the elements, too. [I] feel good about our football team."

He felt good about the second-half adjustments. The Wolverines, who were 0-of-7 on third down in the first half and had 64 yards rushing on 21 carries, finished with 225 yards rushing and averaged 4.5 yards a carry. "It felt like old-fashioned slobber-knocker football," Harbaugh said.

Michigan also blocked two punts for a special teams boost, and the defense held prolific Indiana to 255 yards, including 191 passing. They all felt good about the win and what was next. "We knew because of the elements it would probably be a defensive battle," Peppers said. "We knew that they had a pretty good deep passing game, and they had tempo. So coming out of halftime, I just told the guys, 'How good do you want to be? We've got a real good opportunity to show the world how great we can be.'"

It was the final time the seniors would wear the winged helmet at home in Michigan Stadium. It was an emotional time for the players. Butt sat on the snow-covered field with eye black smeared down his cheeks and he cried. "It kind of hit me then," he said. "I held it in, I held it in, then I was looking around the stadium, and I was like, 'Wow, this is the last time I'm ever going to be in here suited up as a player.' This is a special moment, and I kind of tried to take it all in."

Michigan players will say some of their fondest moments are in the tunnel, on the lip of the field as they prepare to run onto the field and touch the banner. This was the last time the seniors would do that. "Before the game we were all like, 'We can't believe we're touching the banner one last time,'" safety Dymonte Thomas said. "We all came here together, we all grinded together, and we're all leaving together except for a few guys who transferred. When they started playing that video and that sad music, Khalid [Hill] comes to me and is like, 'I might start crying.' I was like, 'If you cry, I'm going to cry.' And JD [Jourdan Lewis] is like, 'What's wrong with y'all? We've got a game. Let's go win.' And then JD is like, 'I might cry too, y'all.' I was like, 'We're going to be all right. Let's go win and make the best of this last year we've got together.'"

Ryan Glasgow said he got sentimental when he saw his parents standing on the sideline holding his jersey before the game. "They were playing some Alicia Keys song to a slideshow of our season," he said. "That was a pretty emotional period. Once you lock into game mode, it's a little different. At the end, it was pretty cool to be out there with all the guys."

Harbaugh knows what it is like to lose your last game at Michigan Stadium as a senior. In 1986 Michigan was ranked No. 2 and was upset by Minnesota 20–17. "It's not a good feeling—at all," he said. "Glad our guys played eight home games and won them all. The constant being a Michigan football player through the ages is that you play in Michigan Stadium in that Big House, always has been that way, is and always will be. That's the one constant of all the time—the facilities, the changes, society, and everything else—you play in that stadium and have that feeling of winning your last game and have it be a big game. It's a great feeling. I feel especially good for them."

18

The Game

T HE MICHIGAN-OHIO STATE GAME WEEK IS ALWAYS unique and so different than any other during the regular season. It is, after all, The Game, arguably the greatest rivalry in sports.

Reporters from Michigan annually make the journey to Columbus, Ohio, for the Ohio State news conference, and reporters from Columbus make their way to Ann Arbor. It is a ritual. Jim Harbaugh stood at the podium and undoubtedly expected questions about quarterback Wilton Speight, who had missed the previous game against Indiana because of an unspecified injury to this left arm, and his guarantee 30 years earlier while quarterback of the Wolverines that Michigan would beat Ohio State in Columbus and go to the Rose Bowl.

But people in Columbus keep a close eye on Michigan—and, since his arrival, Harbaugh. *The Columbus Dispatch*'s separate online section devoted to Ohio State athletics, "buckeyextra," has a feature on the top left: days since Michigan's last win against Ohio State.

Harbaugh may have been puzzled by a question he received the Monday of game week from a *Dispatch* columnist, but for a Michigan-Ohio State week question, it was not unusual: "You're going to a place where they don't know what to make of you. Some say you're crazy like a fox; some say you're just crazy. But they all say you're progressive. Can you describe who you are to Ohioans?"

Harbaugh did not bite. "I'm not crazy," he said. "I wouldn't describe myself as that. I don't know my personality, how relevant that will be in the game this week, probably irrelevant."

The subject didn't die there, however. Harbaugh is a curiosity.

He wears the same outfit all the time, he wears cleats, he wears a hat with a suit, he appears in a rap video. Soon after his arrival in Ann Arbor, he helped rescue a woman who had slid off an icy highway. He challenges the NCAA and he carries his baseball glove to games.

But crazy?

His players who had played for him the last two seasons said that wasn't even close to an accurate description. "He's as real as they come," Erik Magnuson said. "The media maybe paints a bad picture of him sometimes because of his antics, going after referees, and stuff like that. But he'll fight for his players and he's a player's coach in that aspect. He's somebody that you'd run through a wall for. He's pretty similar to what you see in everyday life. That's who he is."

Most of the players subscribe to the approach Harbaugh is an out-of-the-box thinker. "He's not crazy, he just does things different," senior co-captain Chris Wormley said. "When you're a top coach, you set yourself apart from average ones. When you're not average, you do things different than everyone else." Senior Kyle Kalis agreed. "Usually, the most successful people have something off about them that sets them apart from other people," he said. "I think Coach Harbaugh's a really good example of that."

The players were asked to describe Ohio State coach Urban Meyer. "This is how we get in trouble," Magnuson said, laughing. "I'm going to say he's a great coach, great guy." Kalis echoed his teammate for his take on Meyer: "Great guy, I've heard nothing but great things."

Wormley took a more serious tone. "With all the great coaches, you've got to be wired a little differently," he said. "All the great ones do things differently. I'm sure Coach Meyer has done things differently because he's a successful coach. And with Coach Harbaugh, he does things differently."

Harbaugh deflected conversation about his guarantee of Michigan's victory against Ohio State 30 years earlier. Something that happened three decades earlier would obviously have no effect on this game. When he arrived at Michigan as head coach, he rid Schembechler Hall of all the "Beat Ohio" signs and the countdown clocks. The Game is big enough; it doesn't need gimmicks.

But his first meeting with Ohio State as head coach was brutal. The Wolverines were trounced 42–13 by the angry Buckeyes who had been upset the week before by Michigan State.

This would be different, though. It felt like a different week. Michigan was 10–1 and ranked No. 3, and Ohio State was 10–1 and ranked No. 2.

Michigan had lost four straight to its arch rival and 11 of the last 12 games, but for the first time in 10 years—since the monumental 2006 showdown of No. 1 Ohio State versus No. 2 Michigan—The Game had plenty on the line to be decided in the final regular-season matchup. If the Wolverines won, they would earn the Big Ten East title and a berth in the Big Ten championship—they had not won a Big Ten title since 2004—and potentially a spot in the four-team national playoff. If Ohio State won, the Buckeyes would still need Penn State to lose to clinch the East to play for the Big Ten title. "Even if you weren't an Ohio State-Michigan fan, you were tuning in to watch that game," Michigan tight end and co-captain Jake Butt, who grew up in Pickerington, just outside of Columbus, said of the 2006 game. "That will be pretty similar this week, No. 2 versus No. 3, really everything on the line for both teams. It's an absolute must-win game so it's going to be a great atmosphere. Everyone is going to be tuning in to watch this."

The rivalry had been desperate for a return to something close to the 10-Year War, those magical Woody and Bo days, and from the moment Harbaugh was hired, everyone started to feel like the war would be back with him and Urban Meyer. But The Game is about the players, and the Wolverines had been feeling the hype building for weeks. Since the midseason point, reporters had been asking them if they've been keeping an eye on the Buckeyes. The trajectory even then seemed to be that the two teams were on a collision course to reach this moment. "Going through the season from Week 1 to Week 13 now, we've seen them playing very well and we've been playing very well, so the hype has been building up for so long," Wormley said. "Now they're 2 and we're 3. It's been building up for a while. It's pretty cool to be in the position."

After the Wolverines beat Indiana last Saturday to go 8–0 at home, the snow was falling, and the "Beat Ohio!' chants could be heard inside and outside Michigan Stadium. "How romantic was that?" Magnuson said. "It was snowing. The field is white, the crowd is yelling Beat Ohio, we're sitting there, puffing our chest up just like, 'Man, we run this place.' Pretty cool. It's a lot different feeling than the past."

Magnuson explained that in the past they felt like Ohio State was strong, and maybe, just maybe the Wolverines could pull off an upset. The 42–13 loss at Michigan Stadium the previous year still stung. "They basically took away our will, took away our pride," Magnuson said. "We felt we were in it to start the game. I felt like they took it away from us as if we gave up. It's like we felt like we didn't have a chance to come back when they got a good lead. I feel like this year it won't be the case."

Cornerback Jourdan Lewis, like Butt, had an opportunity to leave for the NFL last season. They came back for an experience like this, they said, and the season had far surpassed what they had imagined. "I didn't expect the path we're on right now," Lewis said. "I wanted to come back and go to a Big Ten championship and I didn't know it would be as special as it was. I've never been through this on a collegiate level, and it's very special, and I'm glad I came back."

Although a win against Ohio State might alleviate more than a decade of angst for the Michigan fans, the players were driven by the lose-and-you're-out playoff approach they had adopted. "It's not as important to win this game for what's been going on in the past,"

Butt said. "Really, we just need to win this game for what we have right in front of us right now. That's all we're focused on. We have an unbelievable opportunity to go on the road, compete against a really good team, and we know our whole entire season is on the line. We need to win the game for that reason. This rivalry is going to be relevant. It never won't be relevant. We're not thinking about losing. It's a must-win game. We understand that we have to win this game and we're going to do everything we can to do that. We're not thinking about losing."

Attempts to have Harbaugh talk about his history as a player are usually fairly futile. While on a conference call with Big Ten reporters on Day Two of Michigan-Ohio State week, Harbaugh wouldn't budge when asked specifically about his guarantee and efficiently sidestepped the question with a patented evasive response. As a refresher: as Michigan's starting quarterback in 1986, he guaranteed the Wolverines would win in Ohio Stadium, and they backed him up with a 26–24 victory.

He got a question he liked, though. Instead of being asked about *the* guarantee, Harbaugh was asked if he gives his players guidelines about making predictions or guarantees. "Yeah," Harbaugh said brightly. "All you can offer is your advice and your wisdom. Not so much wisdom, I would say, experience. On that topic I have experience. Thirty years later, I found it not necessary. To make a guarantee, what are you really guaranteeing? I offer that. Having done it, I don't recommend it."

It was a rare bit of humor in a pressure-packed week. There were other storylines making the rounds, ones that didn't affect Harbaugh or Meyer. But because the two rival fanbases share so much—from animosity to history to rivalry—the 2006 game from 10 years earlier resonates.

It was No. 1 Ohio State versus No. 2 Michigan, the only time the two teams have faced each other ranked that high. The death of Bo Schembechler a day before the game was felt across the country but most acutely among Michigan *and* Ohio State fans.

He was an Ohio native who had been an OSU assistant early in his career and was forever linked with legendary OSU coach Woody Hayes. The Buckeyes won that game 42–36 and played for a national championship. "I can't believe it's been 10 years," Jake Long, Michigan's All-American left tackle from that team, said. "To this day that was such an emotional game that had so much riding on it. I remember it every day. It haunts me all the time. But I have no regrets for that game. We played our hearts out. We couldn't have played any better."

This game in 2016, Harbaugh's second shot at coaching against Ohio State, had that heavyweight title match feel just like the game 10 years earlier. One way to identify the hype is how far ESPN is willing to go. *GameDay*, normally a three-hour show setting up the day's games each week, expanded to five hours and would be live from Columbus, and the final 90 minutes of the show would be from inside The Shoe. ESPN sent nearly 250 employees to Columbus to handle every aspect of the broadcast. There would be cameras—a lot of cameras—from those in pylons to those on the goal posts to a SkyCam and super slow motion cameras. Every angle would be covered. "We're pulling out the stops here," Lee Fitting, who oversees studio and game production for ESPN, said in the days before the game. "It's our regular-season Super Bowl, if you will. Our mantra is: when you get an opportunity like this, spare no expense and crush these games."

Fitting said there was a "whole different feel" the day before the 2006 game because of Bo's passing. "What makes it feel a little bit different this time," Fitting said, "is the Harbaugh factor. Coach Harbaugh ratchets it up a little bit. He's just polarizing, and people are intrigued by polarizing figures."

The day before The Game was festive. Every M on the OSU campus and in much of Columbus was replaced with a big red X. The *GameDay* crew was going through its prep work, and Desmond

Howard and Kirk Herbstreit—Howard, the Heisman Trophy winner from Michigan, and Herbstreit, an OSU quarterback, had played in the rivalry—took a break to meet with some local media.

With the Ohio State band across the way practicing and Ohio Stadium off to the right, Howard and Herbstreit both predicted the teams had saved things in their playbook for the next day. On paper, they said, this was a great matchup. Although they shared similar impressions of the game, they differed slightly on how quickly Harbaugh would turn around the program. Howard envisioned this kind of turnaround in Year Two under Harbaugh because of his resume and his track record.

Herbstreit, consistent with what he said before the start of the season, thought it might take a bit longer. "This is what he does. He turns programs around relatively quickly," Howard said. "The most important thing is he's changed the culture. I think that's key. Year Two, ranked No. 3 in the country, it's pretty big, pretty relevant."

Howard is close to his alma mater, is a frequent visitor, and is part of a number of events there throughout the year. He observed the program closely the previous seven years when Rich Rodriguez and then Brady Hoke were at the helm. Harbaugh, in his mind, was the missing piece. "First and foremost, when you get a new coach, it has to be the right fit," Howard said. "I don't care how great this coach is at the program he's coaching. If he's not a great fit for your program, it's just not going to work. As great as Jim Harbaugh is as a coach, he's the right fit for Michigan. He understands the culture, he knows what Michigan football, at least in his mind, looks like, what it's about. He understands the region, he understands the conference. So to me it's not shocking or surprising he's been able to do what he's been able to do in such a short period of time because he's the right fit. I know the media loves to talk about his quirk or that quirk. He's got khakis on, but what they don't criticize him for is what he's getting [done], which is to coach. He's a hell of a coach."

Three months after saying he believed Harbaugh and Michigan

are a year away from making the jump into the upper echelon of college football, Herbstreit remained consistent. He thought it might take a few more recruiting classes for Harbaugh to make the Wolverines competitive in the national picture. "When they hired Jim Harbaugh, we were out at the Rose Bowl, I remember thinking it's not about if—but when—he brings them back," Herbstreit said. "I had the same feelings when Alabama hired Nick Saban. I thought, *Hope you get your shots in now because he's bringing Bama back*, and that's exactly how I feel about Jim Harbaugh.

"I made a comment earlier in this year: Michigan is going to be good this year, but his better teams are ahead of him. That's from a physical, on paper standpoint, not intangibles. This is a unique situation because of having a veteran group, but physically, he's going to recruit better quarterbacks, better wide receivers, better running backs like the type of players that were there throughout the '80s and '90s when they were on fire sending guys to the NFL. That's coming back. I guess I'm surprised because he's inherited this team; they've bought into his culture and the fact they're at the level where they are. I think anybody has to be surprised that it's been this quick. As a fan of the Big Ten and being at Ohio State, I'm a huge fan of him bringing Michigan back because it's healthy for the rivalry, it's great for the Big Ten, and it's great for college football anytime you bring that brand back to where he has brought them."

Both men think Harbaugh and Meyer could be the answer for a return to the 10-Year War. "We're all bracing, hoping we get those two big personalities on both sidelines," Herbstreit said. "I'm part of hoping it's what everyone is hoping for."

The game lived up to the hype. Still hampered by the injury to his left shoulder, Michigan quarterback Wilton Speight had three turnovers but played valiantly, and Ohio State overcame a 10-point deficit in the third quarter to win 30-27 in double overtime. An Ohio Stadium-record crowd of 110,045 witnessed the first overtime game in the history of the rivalry. "This is what you go to Michigan, this is what you go to Ohio State for—to play that team the last regular-season game," Wormley said. "This is the type of exciting game you look back on and talk about with friends and family. I wish we could have gotten that one."

With the loss went the Wolverines' hope of being the Big Ten East representative in the Big Ten championship the following week, and the dream of a playoff appearance had been all but officially denied as the Wolverines finished the season 10–2 while Ohio State finished 11–1.

Harbaugh had been beside himself regarding the officiating throughout the game. But in the second overtime and with Michigan leading 27–24 after a Kenny Allen field goal, his disdain went to a new level. On Ohio State's ensuring series, Michigan believed it had stopped quarterback J.T. Barrett on fourth down. The ball was spotted at the 15-yard line for a first down, and a review upheld the ruling on the field. A play later Curtis Samuel scored on a 15-yard run to win the game.

Harbaugh's postgame interview session became an angry dissection of the officiating, though he never blamed the officiating for the Wolverines' loss. "There wasn't a first down by that much," Harbaugh said, holding his hands about a foot apart. Harbaugh spent most of his postgame news conference lambasting the officials for what he thought were bad calls and missed calls. "I'm bitterly disappointed with the officiating today," he said. "That spot, the graphic displays, the interference penalties. One not called on [Michigan receiver] Grant Perry clearly being hooked before the ball got there. And the previous penalty they called on Delano Hill. The ball is uncatchable by the receiver. So I'm bitterly disappointed in the officiating, can't make that any more clear. My view of the first down is that it was short."

Harbaugh mentioned the discrepancies in the penalties. Ohio State had two for six yards while Michigan was penalized seven times for 59 yards. "Two penalties called all day," he said. "Multiple holding penalties let go, multiple false starts. The official on my side is supposed to be watching that [and instead] is concerned about whether our coaches are in the white or not in the white [of the coaches' box]. He wants us not on the field. Their coaches were on the field practically in the huddle at times. I'm bitter."

Harbaugh and the Michigan sideline also were called for unsportsmanlike conduct after Harbaugh threw his play sheet and hat. He was responding to an offside penalty on Maurice Hurst with which he disagreed. Responding to a question about whether he felt Michigan lost the game or it was taken from them, Harbaugh skewered the officials again. "What do you think? That's what I think," Harbaugh said. "As I said, bitterly disappointed in the officiating. [They] could have been watching the game rather than being concerned about, throwing a hat. If you throw a hat, if you throw a script toward your sideline, that's a penalty? I asked him about it, he said, 'Well, it is in basketball.' I go, 'Well, this isn't basketball.' Well, he told me he officiates basketball. I don't know the relevance. He said it would have been a technical in basketball. I'm bitter."

As reporters filtered out of the room, one recalled how familiar Harbaugh's postgame rant had sounded like Bo Schembechler's comments in 1973 after a vote by the Big Ten athletic directors sent Ohio State, not Michigan, to the Rose Bowl. Schembechler at the time called it a bitter disappointment and would later call it the greatest disappointment of his career.

A few hours afterward, a columnist for *The Detroit News* wrote on Twitter that one of the Big Ten officials—the basketball official Harbaugh referenced—was an Ohio native and had recently been inducted into the Ohio High School Athletic Association Officials Hall of Fame. This sparked a number of conspiracy theories regarding the officiating and the background of the officials who had worked the game. The Big Ten later clarified that there were three officials from Ohio and three from Michigan who worked the game.

Several weeks later, *Chicago Tribune* reporter Teddy Greenstein had a three-hour interview with Bill Carollo, the Big Ten's coordinator of officials, and they discussed some of the calls in that game. Carollo told the *Tribune* that the "ruling was close enough" on the fourth-down spot in the second overtime. Carollo said whatever was called on the field would not have been overturned by replay.

He did admit to one missed call, which he described as an "egregious no-call." That was when Ohio State running back Mike Weber knocked down Michigan cornerback Brandon Watson just as Jabrill Peppers was being tackled after a third-quarter interception. There was no whistle, but Weber's move fell in the category of unnecessary roughness. Carollo, according to the *Tribune*, "downgraded the official who declined to throw the flag."

On the play involving Perry that Harbaugh referenced in his postgame comments, Carollo said "that's a 50-50 call that was not flagged."

In the aftermath of the game, Harbaugh drew a public reprimand and was fined $10,000 by the Big Ten. Several weeks later when asked about the fine, Harbaugh did not seem fazed—or deterred. "I don't accept it as a given that you can't speak your mind or tell the truth," Harbaugh said. "Well, I guess we can all just call it—we see it differently and let it go with that. But I still don't accept it as a given that you can't speak your mind and give your opinion on how you see things."

But that's never *it* with Harbaugh. Never. Ever.

About two weeks after the Michigan-Ohio State game, Los Angeles Rams coach Jeff Fisher was fired. How does this have anything to do with Michigan or Harbaugh? NFL opening equals a Harbaugh-to-the-NFL rumor du jour. The rumor began when Albert Breer, an NFL insider, was on the show, *The Herd with Colin Cowherd*, three days before Fisher was fired. Before the show Breer and Cowherd talked about the Rams pursuing Harbaugh if the firing happened. Breer said to Cowherd in their off-air conversation, "If I am the Rams, the first call I make is Jim Harbaugh."

Breer and Cowherd never discussed that on air, but Cowherd decided to tell his audience that, "By the way Albert Breer, on the way out, said the Jim Harbaugh-to-the-Rams rumor is a very real thing." The rumors spun out of control and heated up after Fisher was fired that Monday. That night Harbaugh told his players after practice he was not leaving Michigan. He told them he had unfinished business in Ann Arbor and then ratcheted it up a notch by telling them the rumors had been perpetuated by college rivals, their "enemies." "He said, 'Look guys, short, sweet to the point, I'm not leaving. Don't worry about it. These are lies made up by our enemies,'" senior defensive lineman Ryan Glasgow said. "It got the team all riled up. We don't want any enemies infiltrating our fortress."

Magnuson, the offensive lineman, clearly had listened to his coach's message and said the Harbaugh rumor mill is fed by rival college programs. "He said he's staying here, he ain't going nowhere," Magnuson said. "He ain't leaving," Kalis, sitting next to best friend Magnuson, chimed in. "He ain't going nowhere," Magnuson said again.

Magnuson and Kalis said this is just another arm of negative recruiting. "For sure," Kalis said. "It's all planned."

Magnuson said people, especially recruits, should not pay attention to the rumors. "A lot of it, unfortunately is just distractions...some of it's by other teams," Magnuson said. "It really hurts recruiting, I think, if they're saying Jim Harbaugh is going into the NFL. Some recruits can think that there's no stability in the coaching job at Michigan, so that can hurt him. A lot of it is created for a distraction in that aspect as far as recruiting. I can't see him going anywhere. This is where he wants to be."

As soon as he started seeing the Harbaugh NFL rumors on social media, Glasgow said he knew there was nothing to them. "I'd see that on Twitter or Facebook and be like, this is just not true.

This is blatantly false," Glasgow said. "We knew just based on how much Coach Harbaugh loves the program, loves Michigan, he's not leaving any time soon—if ever. He could be one of those coaches you see at Michigan 15, 20 years down the line. I don't see him leaving any time soon. He said, 'You're stuck with me.'"

Though Glasgow would be moving on to the NFL after the bowl games, he knows and the other players know that Harbaugh-to-the-NFL rumors will surface every year at this time. "He's a football coach that's probably wanted by a ton of pro and college organizations that are willing to pay him almost anything," Glasgow said. "So yeah, it's probably something that the program is going to have to get used to."

A day after telling his team there was nothing to the rumor, Harbaugh then told a full house of Michigan fans—former players and players' parents at the annual football banquet—the same. It came without prompting. "I'm not leaving Michigan, not even considering it," Harbaugh said to the crowd, which erupted with loud applause. "A lot of this talk is coming from our enemies, from coaches. You know the names. You probably know the names of the top three I'm referring to. They like to say that to the media. They like to tell that to recruits and their families and try to manipulate them into going to some other school besides Michigan. We know them as jive turkeys."

Jive turkeys. This was a new Harbaughism, a hilarious one that became a big part of conversation for the next week. A few weeks later, while appearing on Kentucky basketball coach John Calipari's podcast, *Cal Cast*, he shared more of his views on negative recruiting and, of course, jive turkeys. "As far as the negative recruiting, a lot of that comes from people that have been saying that for six months or a year. They're our enemies, they're our competition," he told Calipari. "They try to manipulate a youngster and their family any way they can. My philosophy and thought on it—if you have to talk about somebody else and somebody else's program and negative

227

recruit them or their situation, then you're really not concentrating on your own program and the situation you have at your school. That's what you should be presenting and that's what you should be encouraging a youngster to look at, not the negative side of recruiting. Definitely people use that against you and they use that against me, and I've long referred to those type of people as jive turkeys."

19

The Orange Bowl

T HE STING OF NOT MAKING IT INTO THE FOUR-TEAM College Football Playoff wasn't quite gone, but it had dulled. The players knew their hopes had dimmed after losing to Ohio State, but they still believed they were one of the nation's top four teams. When Clemson and Washington won their conference championship games—a loss by either may have given Michigan a chance to slide into the playoff—the reality set in.

Michigan was set for an Orange Bowl matchup against Florida State and a shot at an 11-win season, which would be the Wolverines' sixth since 1905. "Eleven wins is kind of a big deal," senior defensive lineman Ryan Glasgow said. "Nine wins is pretty good, 10 wins and you're getting there. Once you get to 11 or 12, I feel you're one of the marquee programs in the nation."

The Wolverines would follow the blueprint from the previous season's bowl trip, which seemed to work just fine. Michigan had beaten Florida 41–7 in the New Year's Day Capital One Bowl, holding the Gators scoreless in the final three quarters. Jim Harbaugh did not want them to vary from the in-season game-week script, so his first bowl with the team was dubbed a business trip. The Orange Bowl approach would follow suit. "I don't think anyone really approaches a bowl game like Coach Harbaugh and the rest of this staff," quarterback Wilton Speight said. "I know we'll be focused and ready to go just like last year. It puts you in the best opportunity to win. Anything you do in life, you should have a business-type approach in my opinion. Be mature, realize the opportunities you have, and take full advantage of them."

Bowl game preparations give coaches a chance to think about the future and give younger players, who maybe didn't get as many focused reps in practice during the season, more individual work. There was considerable talk about the potential drop-off on defense, considering so many players no longer had eligibility and would be moving on. The departing veterans brimmed with confidence that the future would be bright, and the defensive line got a boost when Maurice Hurst announced he would return for his final season. Following suit, fullback Khalid Hill announced he also planned to return, giving the offense another veteran in the backfield who would be back in 2017. Although coaches and players looked toward the 2017 spring and in a broader spectrum the upcoming season, business is business, and the focus was Florida State in the Orange Bowl.

Bowl games always schedule events for the team, and this was no different. There would be an excursion to Miami Beach, a bowl-arranged dinner at a mall restaurant, and another all-you-can-eat meal, but for the Michigan Wolverines, the Orange Bowl was much more than that.

They wanted to prove they were worthy of being in the four-team playoff, a goal they had set before the season, and 11 wins would show tangible improvement from Harbaugh's first season as coach when they went 10–3. "It's a business trip," Hill said. "A lot of teams go in thinking, *Oh, okay, we're going to go on vacation.* It's a bowl game. You get to go to a different place and play someone else. It's a business trip as Coach Harbaugh says. You get to have fun after the game. We'll be as serious as possible. Last year, we took it very seriously. There was no going out. It was straight books, in your hotel room and practice. That was it."

Winning a bowl game often translates to momentum heading into the next season. The Michigan players, who returned after the victory against Florida, definitely found it gave them a charge as they got into winter conditioning and into spring practice. "It means everything," Hurst said. "It puts a nice taste in your mouth. I've been there before where we lost to Kansas State [after the 2013 season], and you have that bitter taste in your mouth the entire offseason. You lost that game and you didn't only lose; you got beat pretty bad. It puts a poor taste in your mouth. Beating Florida, we had that positive attitude going throughout camp and throughout everything, knowing we were playing our best football toward the end of the year and kind of keep the ball rolling. I think it's great momentum going into the offseason to prove you're a great team and that your best football is yet to come."

Although many national college football analysts debated whether the four-team playoff had devalued the rest of the bowls, the Orange is a New Year's bowl and still considered prominent. It was one more opportunity to play, one more opportunity for Michigan to prove something against a strong opponent. "We're going out with a bang, showing everybody what our preparation was," cornerback Channing Stribling said. "I don't care what bowl game it is. I'll still be happy to play. We still have to prepare for this game like it's still a national championship game."

Michigan lost two of its final three games by a total of four points. The Wolverines knew how close they were to breaking into that elite, elite group, and that was their motivation heading into the business trip. This game also gave the older players more time to reflect on where the program had been and how far it had come in two years. Although the Orange Bowl was a disappointment in one sense, it was also a sign of the improvement the program had made under Harbaugh and his staff. "The Orange Bowl is a big game," Glasgow said. "We're happy to play in the game. It's just not where we wanted to be at this point in the season. We're not going to take it for granted. Two years ago we might not even be able to fathom that we'd be here at this point. We're happy to be in the Orange Bowl but not quite satisfied, I think is a good way to put it."

College campuses are often in the middle of political debates, and the most recent presidential election stirred plenty of controversy and discussion. Michigan backup quarterback John O'Korn said students were emotionally drained after Donald Trump won the election, and some were so distraught they didn't attend classes. Football players and athletes across campuses are in a bubble, to be sure, but they are not isolated and certainly not immune to current events.

Harbaugh makes it a point to facilitate and encourage conversation among the players on a number of issues. "He's not just in that way but in so many ways such a unique coach because he's played," O'Korn said. "There are so many coaches who coach college football who have never played a day of college football in their lives. He's experienced it himself. That affects how he coaches, how he leads. It says a lot about him as a person. There have been so many discussions about a number of issues he's started off a meeting or ended a practice talking about."

After the team's final practice in Ann Arbor before departing for Florida, Harbaugh, joined by athletic director Warde Manuel, opened discussion with the players about their Orange Bowl-assigned hotel, the Trump National Doral in Miami. "Naturally, there were a lot of emotions and opinions about this decision," O'Korn said. "Everyone shared their opinions on it. We ended up staying there and we had a great time, we had a great bowl trip, but we had that discussion. It was open for the entire team. People shared their opinions on both sides. That discussion had to be had before we went down there, or else there would have been a huge uproar once we got there."

With the air cleared and the players grateful their coach was willing to discuss the issue, the Wolverines were prepared to head to Miami to handle their business trip. There is always a different feel to a bowl trip for the seniors. Although they had already gone through their final home game playing in the winged helmet and their final Ohio State game, the bowl is it—the final game of their college careers. As they got closer to the game, the players started to understand this would be it, the last time they played together as a group.

Chris Wormley, a co-captain and starting defensive lineman who is not the most emotional of the players, had started to consider what's next. He would start training for the NFL draft after the bowl, but the idea of moving on from Michigan wasn't something he chose to dwell on. "I know maybe in a couple weeks or a month or so when I'm off training somewhere it'll hit me that this team will never be the same. I'll never put on that winged helmet again," Wormley said in late December of 2016. "But right now I'm just enjoying Miami, enjoying being with the guys for three more days, so it really hasn't sunk in yet."

Harbaugh had been in this position as a player and as a coach. He lives and breathes football, but being part of a team, coaching a team is what drives him. Coaching is teaching, and teaching is about as organic as it gets in terms of communicating and shaping individuals. Admittedly, he felt the emotions of the week. "I get very sentimental," Harbaugh said a day before the game. "I understand that the team won't be the same. When this game is over, it'll exist in the record books, it'll exist in our memories, but the ball team, as we know it, won't be the same after this game. So I get very nostalgic about that. I want them to leave with dignity and pride, knowing that they went out and played the very best they could and gave it their all. That's all you can ask, and we'll strive for that to be a win."

Harbaugh said this large senior class, which had such high aspirations this season of winning a Big Ten championship and earning a spot in the College Football Playoff, had practiced for the bowl with a sense of urgency. A victory against Florida State would mean 11 wins, rarefied air for the program, a second straight bowl victory under Harbaugh, and perhaps a top five final ranking. A group of seniors that had set the bar so high and come up short during the regular season was now facing a final game. "You're never in anybody else's skin but your own, but I've looked back and I remember sitting in locker rooms and peewee hockey and little league football and baseball and knowing that that was going to be my last hockey game or my last high school football game or last high school basketball game, last college game, you know, different times throughout my own life," Harbaugh said. "It's understood by our players that that's the situation. They're playing their last college game. For many of our senior players that are going through their last game at Michigan, it's a last time to be with your team, to connect with your teammates. This team will never be the same team again after this ballgame. Young players and those players that are continuing at the University of Michigan playing for the Wolverines, this is a chance to continue to be with their teammates and build the most important relationship that you have on a football team with your teammates. Just taking advantage of that tremendous opportunity is the way we've been approaching it."

The players said they had not done much during the week in Miami. Most opted not to go to a few of the functions and didn't venture to the beach. This trip would not be about goofing around and wasting time. Kyle Kalis said he was asleep by 11:00, about a half hour before bed check each night. Harbaugh did not quite embrace the business trip description, though. For him, any game week is about the business of winning. "You say 'all-business approach,'" Harbaugh said. "That doesn't resonate with me. This connecting with our team, being with our team, doing what we love to do, we're doing it for the last time for some guys. Others, it's maybe the second time or the first time. But to have the opportunity to be around your teammates, and when you're on a team, those relationships that you have with your teammates, those are the tightest ones, those are the closest ones. That's the way I feel about it and approach it."

The bowl practices and entire experience, while sentimental at times for Harbaugh, also allowed him to look forward to the upcoming spring practice and development of his next team. He did not share impressions of players who stood out, but he was encouraged despite knowing there was plenty of work ahead. "There's obvious improvements that need to be made," Harbaugh said. "That's a process, and it gives you a better idea for when spring practice starts [that] here's the areas that we need to address with some of the younger players. But that's always a heck of a good time to start. You feel like you've got to jump on it, and I feel like you've cheated the system, that the young players are getting the opportunity to have spring practice before spring practice even starts. That process has begun."

The future could wait, though. This was about making Orange Bowl memories for his players and himself. Harbaugh tells stories about being a kid on bowl trips with his father and family. He and his brother were always running around having a ball, and it overjoyed him to see his children doing the same. Five of his then-six children were on the trip, including Jay Harbaugh, of course, since he's an assistant coach.

His young son, Jack, came to one of the last practices and told his father that was the highlight of the trip. "It warmed my heart," Harbaugh said. "You know, just watching our families—not just mine but other coaches' sons, daughters that have come to practice or been around the team meals interacting with the team—watching our players interact with my kids is great. They've been awesome. I remember that feeling as a kid when a Michigan football player would notice me as a nine or 10-year-old and pat you on the back or toss you a ball, and to see Jake [Butt] or John O'Korn tossing the ball with my kids, it's like you fight back the tears. You get very sentimental. I do. It's as good as it gets."

The pregame dance between the two teams was predictable, of course. Michigan spoke highly of the Seminoles' highly lauded running back Dalvin Cook, who was ranked seventh nationally in rushing yards. Many thought he should have been a Heisman Trophy finalist. Florida State exchanged the compliments, heaping praise on Michigan's defense, which entered the game ranked second nationally in yardage (an average of 252.7 yards per game), second in scoring defense (12.5 points), first in pass defense (135.9 yards), and 13th against the run (116.8 yards). "It's ridiculous what they've accomplished," Randy Sanders, FSU's co-defensive coordinator said before the game. "[This is] probably one of the better [defenses] I've faced in my 28, 29, I don't even know how many years I've been coaching. But to play a team like this with 10 seniors starting on defense, and the only junior is Jabrill Peppers, that's pretty unusual. In the late '80s, early '90s, you might play a team that had 10 seniors, but I can't remember the last time we played a defense with 10 seniors starting."

It was a beautiful night for the Orange Bowl on December 30 at Hard Rock Stadium. The sky had been a mix of a glowing yellow against a blue backdrop that evolved into a burning orange and purple sunset. Inside, the crowd was roughly 70 percent Florida State fans and 30 percent Michigan.

The rumors started early that Michigan's Heisman Trophy finalist and team MVP Peppers would miss the game because of a hamstring injury. He took the field for pregame warmups and very gingerly tried to stretch his left side. He tried to work through it, but he was ruled out by game time.

Florida State started fast, and the Wolverines, who wanted to use this game to prove they were worthy of being in the national playoff, looked flat. They tried to overcome a 14-point deficit and the loss of two top players, Peppers and tight end Jake Butt, who suffered a torn knee ligament early in the game. But despite two fourth-quarter touchdowns and a late lead, Michigan's vaunted defense could not get a critical stop on a final FSU drive set up by a big kickoff return.

The Wolverines, who at one point were 9–0 and ranked No. 2 nationally, lost 33–32. They lost three of their final four games by a total of five points. It was a crazy finish, and Speight said it reminded him of the double-overtime loss at Ohio State. "I didn't think that Ohio State [game] would be topped," Speight said. "It probably isn't because that was Ohio State, but both were just roller-coaster type games. But you know, the past games we came up [five] points short. Wow. We play this game for games like those [five] points. We're just on the wrong end of them."

Michigan took its first lead of the game with 1:57 left when freshman running back Chris Evans ran 30 yards for a touchdown, and Speight connected with Amara Darboh on the two-point conversion. That gave the Wolverines a 30–27 lead, and they felt confident. "That drive was awesome, and that two-point conversion, I was like, 'That's it. That's the nail in the coffin,'" Speight said. "The whole Michigan corner was electric."

But Florida State wasn't done. Keith Gavin returned the kickoff 66 yards before Jourdan Lewis made a touchdown-saving tackle. After FSU took a timeout with 42 seconds left, it scored to take a 33–30 lead. "I thought he was kneeing the ball on that kick return," Speight said. "I was like, 'Oh, that's a great kick Kenny.' [Gavin] hesitated, which I think made our kickoff guys hesitate or something. It's not just that play. It's a bunch of different plays."

And just when you'd think it couldn't have gotten more hectic, it did. Michigan's Chris Wormley blocked the extra point, and Josh Metellus picked it up and returned it for two, cutting FSU's lead to 33–32 and got the ball back with 36 seconds left. "It's a good feeling, getting a block and then having Josh return that for those two points to put us at a one-point deficit," Wormley said. "But we knew we had to make another stop. Our offense had to get the ball back. So at the end of the day, we knew we had to score again to win the game, so our focus was getting the ball back to the offense in a good position to win."

The Wolverines' last-ditch effort ended when Speight, who had been under heat from what he called the best defensive front he had seen all season, threw an interception on fourth down. "I don't think we came out flat," Speight said. "They just came out playing really well and firing on all cylinders. You see boxing, you see UFC stuff, maybe even golf, you come out, you're doing the right things, but the other team comes out hot, the fighter comes out hot. You take the punch, roll with it, and move on, and that's what we did."

Michigan finished the season 10–3 for the second straight year under Harbaugh.

"I love them, love these guys," Michigan coach Jim Harbaugh said, "great group of competitors, great group of workers, and a great group of guys that find a way. They've got a will to win. Not just they want to win; I mean, they must win. I love them for it."

Not having Peppers, the Big Ten's Defensive Player of the Year, and Butt made an enormous dent in Michigan's gameplan. Butt, the Mackey Award winner as the nation's best tight end, injured his right knee after making a 16-yard reception in the second quarter. He writhed in pain but eventually walked off the field without assistance, though he had a slight limp. With a towel over his head, he walked to the locker room and gave a thumbs up to Michigan fans in the stands as he passed.

This was the second time in his college career that Butt had torn his ACL. He suffered the first injury in February of 2014. "I talked to him at halftime. I told him I love him," Speight said. "I credit a lot of how I bounce from adversity through how I watched him. He took me under his wing immediately and I watched from afar how he operated. He had an ACL a couple years ago that I watched him bounce back from with ease. I don't know if that's what happened tonight. Whatever happened, I know he's going to bounce back better than everybody."

Peppers sat in the Michigan locker room after the game fighting back tears. He sounded emotional as he discussed how difficult it was to sit out the Orange Bowl because of a hamstring injury suffered a day earlier in practice. Most thought it would be the last time Peppers would play in a Michigan uniform, and he confirmed that a few weeks later when he announced his intentions to make himself available for the NFL draft. "Everything that happened will work into that decision, not just this game," Peppers said of weighing his options. "I still feel like I didn't do all that I set out to do as an individual and a team. We didn't make the playoffs. We didn't make the Rose Bowl. Coming and losing the Orange Bowl just sucks. We worked so hard for it. We worked too hard to come away with nothing."

Harbaugh had explained that Peppers hurt himself the day before the game. "Jabrill had a hamstring grab on him," Harbaugh said. "He was jumping for a ball. It was very unfortunate. He wasn't able to run, could see it on the film yesterday, and he couldn't get to where he could run and be effective out there, so we didn't play him."

Peppers said he tried to go in pregame warmups, but he was too limited. "Every time I tried to extend my leg up, there was a sharp sensation," he said. "They wrapped it in Icy Hot. I didn't want to hurt the team. I was just going to slow the team down. I'm used to playing a certain way, a certain play style. They told me to see how I felt after warmups when I get the adrenaline pumping, and your body gets warm and loose. It loosened up a little bit, but it wasn't enough to play. I felt if this game was Saturday, I'd definitely play in this game. You hurt a hamstring one day before a game, man, no matter who you are, it's going to be tough."

He said after being hurt his freshman year he applied for insurance. "I don't think anybody knows about that process," he said. "After my freshman year and I got hurt, I didn't care about getting hurt anymore, not only because I had insurance, but I had a football team to win for. I just stopped taking everything for granted. I could care less about what people think about why I didn't play. Not being out there with my brothers, that hurts more than the loss."

Peppers was not on the sideline during the game, a decision, he said, that was made by Harbaugh. "I wanted to be on the sideline,"

Peppers said. "Coach Harbaugh made me go upstairs to the press box. I think he said it would be like a spectacle or something like that. It was best if I was up in the press box. I was doing whatever I could up there, doing what I could to help the team, helping with personnel, things like that."

As he spoke to reporters, Peppers was emotional and said he had many thoughts going through his mind. "This sucks we couldn't send these seniors out the right way," he said. "It sucks I couldn't help the team. We worked too hard. I feel the season was, all the hard work we put it in, the seniors definitely deserved better than this. Not being able to play sucks."

After the game the right side of Speight's lip was cut and slightly swollen, and his white road uniform was covered with grass stains. The quarterback said the Seminoles' defensive line was the best he's faced. FSU sacked him four times, and Michigan allowed 15 tackles for loss. "Those guys were freaks," Speight said. "But we were able to stand our ground and hang with them."

But as he thought about the season, his first as the full-time starter, there was the disappointment of being on such a roll before the tight losses at Iowa and Ohio State and then, of course, in the bowl game. A team that had dreamed so big, as Harbaugh always preaches, could not fulfill all of its goals. "That's tough to look back on the season—a five-point swing from being undefeated," Speight said. "That's tough, but that's life. That's 100 percent life. The coaches know that, the guys know that. We're grown men now. There's no saying, 'Gosh, I wish we could get five points back.' That's the way the cookie crumbles I guess."

Less than a month after the season, Harbaugh made an appearance on ESPN Chicago's *Waddle and Silvy* show. They asked him how long it took him to get over the Ohio State loss. "I can't remember," he said. "A while."

Harbaugh wants to take the program to the elite level and he said the three losses in the final four games made him ask a key question. "How do we make this so we win these type of games?" Harbaugh said. "I don't know if it's ever really good to ever get over it. My thing is: let's keep reminding ourselves. Let's make that: make us better. Hey, sometimes you don't get the pay raise, sometimes you don't get the job promotion, sometimes you don't win the game. Good. Let's use that to make us better."

He was asked if his job at Michigan is everything he thought it would be. He became thoughtful about what could have been in his second season with the Wolverines. "I'm enjoying the heck out of it," he said. "It's everything and more. It's been great, not everything great. Even the things that haven't been good, like we lost three out of our last four games, two by one point and one by three points in overtime. They were excruciating losses but really close to being perfect. As close to being perfect as any team I've ever been on without being perfect. And my thought is good. Good. That will make us more hungry. That will make us more motivated. That will make us work that much harder to be better, to be the best we can possibly can. I like that."

Epilogue

WHAT HAS JIM HARBAUGH DONE IN TWO SEASONS coaching his alma mater? It depends what exactly you want to measure and how you want to measure it. The facts are clear—the Wolverines have had two straight 10-win seasons, a steep improvement from the previous seven seasons, in which the program had only four winning seasons. Michigan, though, finished third in the Big Ten East in both seasons and still has not won a conference title since 2004. Things had looked promising for the Wolverines in 2016, but three losses in the final four games by a total of five points separated a remarkable season from a very good double-digit win season.

But for those who sat through the miserable final home game against Maryland in 2014 and for the players who then spent the next month without a coach and not knowing their future and that of the program, Harbaugh has restored the ability of Michigan fans to puff out their chests a bit and to be excited again. Harbaugh is about expectations. He frequently talks about winning all the trophies and awards that are available, and there are plenty of those. Perhaps highest among those goals and expectations is beating Ohio State, something the Michigan program has done twice since 2001.

And while there is plenty of room for growth and ground to make up to re-establish Michigan consistently among the nation's elite, so much already has been done. "Coach Harbaugh has done so much in a lot of different areas," former Texas coach and current ESPN college football analyst Mack Brown said. "I like a lot of the moves he's made that have brought attention to his program. Everyone is talking about them. Jim is making a push to making Michigan the cool place to be."

EPSN's Kirk Herbstreit said before the 2016 season that while he saw an improving Michigan program under Harbaugh, he believed the Wolverines were still just on the outside of contending for a national title. Look toward 2017, he said, pointing out that Michigan would have its rivalry games against Michigan State and Ohio State at Michigan Stadium. More importantly, Herbstreit pointed out, Harbaugh would have yet another recruiting class of his players coming into the program. And the way Michigan had been recruiting, that could mean only positive things for the Wolverines, he said.

Back-to-back 10-win seasons, though, caught Brown a bit off guard. "They're way ahead of where I thought they would be," Brown said. "To me, they're way ahead of schedule. Obviously, Brady [Hoke] had some good players. The question is, can you win all the games without a superstar quarterback without experience? What they've done—they've taken a transfer from Iowa [Jake Rudock in 2015] and won 10 and took another quarterback [Wilton Speight in 2016] that people really hadn't heard of and started the year without great numbers and continued to get better and better and better. That's been what's impressive to me."

Harbaugh, he said, is building Michigan to last. "They're a little like Alabama in that Coach Harbaugh is building a team of great balance that can run and throw," Brown said. "He made a great hire in Don Brown, and it's no surprise to me he had the success he had at Michigan that he did at Boston College. I would think just watching all the games in two years, Jim is much further ahead than I would have thought in two years."

Jake Butt, whose great honor he said was being a co-captain of the 2016 team, has never been surprised by how far the program was able to grow under Harbaugh. "Once Coach Harbaugh came in and brought in his staff, he kind of gave us this vision and showed us the way a little bit where we started to really believe, too, that this can be something really great."

They saw how much Harbaugh was willing to work to start bringing Michigan back, and Butt said the players responded. "He's going to push us really hard and work us really hard," Butt said. "I'm confident in saying we're one of the hardest practicing teams in the country just because of the way he sets it up. You've heard about the four-hour practices and the two-a-days and the meetings and the long days at camp, but there's a method to his madness. He just wants to see us succeed. He wants to see his team reach its full potential and he doesn't want to leave that up to chance. He's going to do everything in his power to make sure that we can get there. We see that, too. And we respect that. We love that we have a coach that cares for us and is going to fight for us."

What the players get from Harbaugh is a coach who will push them just as Bo Schembechler had once pushed him. "As a coach he's everything you want," Jabrill Peppers said. "He gets the best out of you, he takes you places you can't take yourself. He's going to challenge you. He's going to coach you hard. As an athlete you need that."

Jim Hackett moved on as Michigan's interim athletic director to a position as chairman of Ford Smart Mobility and handed the reigns to Warde Manuel. Hackett wasn't part of the day-to-day operations, but he was focused on Michigan's season in 2016 as a former player and athletic director. And he has never ceased being amazed by Harbaugh's creativity. When Hackett introduced Harbaugh at his introductory news conference on December 30, 2014, he referenced Paul Brown. Harbaugh reminded him of Brown because of the success he had had at the college and NFL levels, understanding, of course, that Brown also had been a highly successful high school coach at Massillon Washington High in Ohio.

But Brown's reach extended beyond the X's and O's. He created the playbook and invented the modern facemask. He was the first to experiment with putting a microphone in the helmet to communicate with quarterbacks. "He was one of the most extraordinary innovators, and this guy we have at Michigan is like that," Hackett said, referring to Harbaugh. "When I heard my dad talk about Brown, I now see it in this coach. [Harbaugh's] always thinking about the construct of the game and ways to win it, all parts of it. I have a feeling it's once-a-generation, these types of instincts. Look how far ahead he was in the camp structure and the practice schedule he put together for the spring. It was a Rubik's Cube of the highest order. He wanted to honor their academics and to build that schedule. He spent a lot of time on that. It was pure genius crafting that. The decision to use the field time instead of [football] class time in the spring, he had to think of a way to improve because his team hadn't been in a bowl game. It explains some of the progress he's made that people didn't expect."

Not quite a year removed from being interim athletic director, Hackett is hesitant to reveal too much regarding his relationship with Harbaugh. "The bond is pretty thick," he said. "I don't want to trivialize the relationship. It's too personal."

The story has been told many times that Michigan players would tape the young Harbaugh boys, Jim and John, into the open lockers as a joke. Hackett appealed to Harbaugh's deep roots at Michigan and encouraged him to revive a program that needed a paddles-to-the-chest spark and get the enthusiasm beating again among the players and the fanbase. "I said to him, 'Jim, I'm starting down a path here, trying to figure out what to do, and you're the first guy I'd like to talk to about this,'" Hackett said. "We didn't talk about the job. We talked about Michigan philosophically, what Michigan needed, and how we both saw it. These talks were just spectacular. It was so easy. It was incredible because of his zest for life and how he sees people and values them. It was really easy. It was a similar philosophy about things. I was surprised actually how aligned we are and still are [considering the] difference in generation. And he was a football coach, and I was a business guy."

Hackett won't take credit for his work in getting the momentum going in the Michigan football program. "I was committed to the success of it, so I'm proud of that," he said. "I didn't want to be denied what was best for Michigan. That's the way I thought about it. It wasn't Jim Hackett; it was Michigan. This was a cause for me. That does feel good. There were people who had lost faith in our history and our unique position and how monumental the university is in some of the things it has achieved. This is an area where it has been monumental."

He said he is proud of Harbaugh and the coaches and feels good about the program's direction, especially considering how low it had dipped. Now, Hackett said, Michigan football is seeing the light, and he's feeling a sense of contentment. "This period that was so tenuous has turned out to be very solid," Hackett said. "We have more work to do. Jim's driven, like me, so you take this advantage to the next level. He's demonstrating yet again with recruiting. He's starting to get the commitments that are going to put us at the top. I feel like we're back."

For Jack Harbaugh, he is back. He has returned to Ann Arbor where he and wife, Jackie, raised their sons during their pivotal high school years. Their sons had a chance to be around the Michigan program as kids and ran around the building and the football fields and got to know Bo Schembechler, who, Jack said, would get down on his knees to talk to the kids eye-to-eye. As Jack commemorated Schembechler on the 10th anniversary of his passing, he could not help but wonder what Bo would think of Jim Harbaugh coaching the Wolverines.

Remember the old story that Jack and Bo used to tell? The two men had played racquetball one day, and in the room where the coaches dressed, there was a desk in the corner by Schembechler's locker. They walked in, and there was young Jim sitting there with his feet on the desk. "Jimmy! You got your feet up on my desk!" Schembechler said.

"Yeah, Bo, I do," Jim Harbaugh said, and kept his feet there.

As Jack tells the story, Schembechler looked at him and said, "Jack, there's something about that kid I really like."

All these years later, Jack wondered what Schembechler would think. "As we watch Jim coach games and go into his office, I look at him sitting across the desk and I smile to myself," Jack Harbaugh said. "And I think, *God, I would love for Bo to be here and be able to watch this.* Just to hear what his comments would be. There would be a lot of comments because he was so honest. If he sees something that could be better, he's going to tell you. You can let your mind drift and wander and put him in that place I could almost picture it. I could do a pretty good job of imagining him. He'd be so proud but would say, 'Jimmy, what were you thinking?' That would be the opening for the discussion. 'Tell me what were you thinking.'"

The seniors, who had weathered the tough times and then the Harbaugh times, were thinking about their legacy as they played their final games for the Wolverines. They didn't win a Rose Bowl or a national championship or a Big Ten title. So what had they accomplished? "Two years ago we were sitting in a team meeting room wondering who our next coach would be, and you look at where we are now, what we've built here. It's satisfying in that sense," Butt said. "The confidence is in those guys, the confidence is in Coach Harbaugh, the confidence is in the identity of this program now. We're not going to go into a season or a game unprepared. We're not leaving something up to chance."

Butt said he and his teammates had laid a foundation during the past two seasons. They helped prepare Michigan for the success they believe will come. "That's the mentality and identity of this program now," he said. "We're not going to talk about it, we're going to be about it. We know that. I think people from the outside looking in know that Michigan is back where it was and where it needs to be and where it will be for a long time."

Being back doesn't mean being done. There is still plenty of work to do, games to win, championship trophies to hold, but those who have been through the first two seasons with Harbaugh said they have every reason to believe the future is bright, and everyone has witnessed the rebirth of Michigan football. "The next three, four, five years, Coach Harbaugh is going to be doing some very special things around here, and he's already started to do that," said Chris Wormley, a co-captain in 2016. "I'm just happy to be part of the process and be a part of the beginning stages of it."

Harbaugh knows there is plenty to do and more four-hour spring practices and more recruiting and just more of more. He said it all in his football treatise. "We will never accept mediocrity at the University of Michigan," Harbaugh wrote in his book. "We never settle for 'good enough.'"

Harbaugh doesn't settle and he certainly doesn't sit still. During the recruiting process that culminated on Signing Day in 2017, Harbaugh had wooed recruits by taking one of his young daughters on a visit and riding go-carts with the recruit. During another visit one recruit's swim team teammates asked to take a photo with him, and Harbaugh insisted on wearing swim caps and goggles in the picture.

He also did not let the NCAA deter him from evolving the IMG spring break trip in 2016 to something more significant and eye-popping. While flying from Detroit to Baltimore in June, 2016, a bigger, better idea came to him. Why not take the team to—Italy?

It took nine months of planning, but Harbaugh finalized plans to take the team in late April to Rome where they would practice three times and spend the rest of the time going to the opera and the Vatican and visiting military and a refugee camp. So the trip would double as practice and a study-abroad-type trip. From Rome many of the players planned to tour on their own and then begin three-week study abroad programs in mid-May. A donor would underwrite the cost of the trip.

But he has thought beyond that. Harbaugh already has plans to take the team to South Africa in Year Two, then Japan, Israel, and either New Zealand or London in Year 5. "It's an unbelievable opportunity for all of us, the youngsters and adults alike, to have an educational opportunity to connect people from another country, to study in terms of study abroad," Harbaugh said. "Most all our players are going to have the opportunity to study abroad, do internships, do service. We're going to Italy for a week. We're going to practice, but from there all our players are going to be able to branch out all over the world. The world is our classroom. They're going to be going to Iceland, Belgium, Japan, Israel, South America, Puerto Rico, all over the world to do their classes. It's so phenomenal. We can't wait to get there."

Many of the players have never left the United States, but they looked forward to the opportunity. For former players, like receiver Braylon Edwards, the idea of a trip like this when he was at Michigan was, well, foreign. But he liked the idea and Harbaugh's out-of-the-box thinking and pointed to the fact that Harbaugh is coaching in a new age where the players are different than when he played. "It's a different age," Edwards said. "He's a huge-picture type of guy. You see what he's doing for recruiting, you see what he's doing for marketing. He's winning on all aspects. I love what he's doing from all standpoints. Everything now with kids is bright lights. It's action, it's big, it's Instagram, it's Twitter, it's material. It's things they can see, things they can hold onto, things they can be happy about or show somebody or tweet about it or text about. So when you do things like taking kids to Rome, that's something I'd be talking about on Twitter, that's something I'd talk about on Instagram. Everything is about projecting a message like, 'Hey, we do it bigger and better than everybody.' That's what he's doing."

Acknowledgments

When I first started covering Michigan football forever ago, in 1992, Bruce Madej was running Michigan's sports information office. He helped introduce me to my new world by taking in Big Ten road games, really, in the only appropriate way—by sampling the best steakhouses in each town. Those were the days. The Big Ten Beef Tour. Bruce called me about writing this book, suggested it would be a good thing to do. In so many ways, this feels like it has all come full circle. Thank you, Bruce. Let's go have a steak.

This would never have happened or been completed without *The Detroit News*, my employer since 1990. The large majority of the reporting for this book is a by-product of my Michigan football beat work for *The Detroit News*, which has always given me the tools to do my job. Any reporting not my own has appropriately been attributed in the text of the book to the respective news outlets.

My job would be more difficult on a daily basis without the help of Dave Ablauf, Michigan's associate athletic director for communications. Dave has for years helped fulfill my interview requests and has always been available when a response is needed on any Michigan football-related topic—even the ones he'd rather not have to deal with. I respect his work ethic and consider him a great friend.

The college football season is a long one, and these days it goes way beyond the fall. With Jim Harbaugh now as the head coach, trust me, the beat has become a 24/7 endeavor. But during the fall (and, of course, the rest of the year), I feel incredibly fortunate to work with the two best columnists in the city of Detroit, Bob Wojnowski and John Niyo of *The Detroit News*. They keep gamedays light when the stress is heavy and then write tremendous copy.

And on that note, a special thanks to *News* sports editor Jim Russ, who is always eager for Michigan football stories and is a great sounding board for story ideas and information. I owe plenty to the great *News* copy editors and colleagues like Tony Paul and James Hawkins who have frequently dropped by Ann Arbor to give me an assist. And much thanks to sports editor Jim Russ who always listens to me talk endlessly about Michigan football.

Phil Laciura deserves a huge amount of thanks. Without him, I would not have this job. Laciura retired as *News* sports editor at the end of 2016, a very tough moment for me. He brought me back to the News four years after I was a college intern and gave me the Michigan football and auto racing beats. He also assigned me to every major sporting event in the city or involving the Detroit teams. It isn't often people work for great bosses—I was lucky.